Turning Point

Turning Points * Vicky Kaseorg

Copyright Vicky Kaseorg 2012

All rights reserved

ISBN-10:1480049522

Turning Points

The life of A WWII Milne Bay Gunner

BY

VICKY KASEORG

2 Corinthians 4:18 (NIV)

So we fix our eyes not on what is seen, but on what is unseen, since what is seen is temporary, but what is unseen is eternal.

Acknowledgements

I would like to thank the friends and loved ones who agreed to read my manuscript several times, and helped me hone my message. I am indebted to my father, John B. Ceccherelli, my brother, John C. Ceccherelli, and my friend Pam Donoghue for taking the time to read, offer suggestions, and cheer me on. I am especially grateful to Comer Hawkins, for entrusting me with his story, and especially with his friendship.

Turning Points * Vicky Kaseorg

Prologue

by Comer Hawkins

Milne Bay Gunner- WWII

In the seventy years that have passed of my life, I have often been asked, "Were you in the services?"

"Yes," I would reply, "In a most important and dangerous theatre of the South Pacific campaign- Milne Bay, New Guinea."

"Where is that?" everyone asks.

I was amazed that so many Americans did not know where New Guinea was! And beyond that, no one knew of Milne Bay. The Battle of Milne Bay was the most decisive and important battle of the South Pacific war. It can be said that it was the battle that saved Australia. Had the Battle at Milne Bay been lost, it would have been a historical disaster for the whole world.

The Japanese forces would literally have walked into Australia. This was the first and only Japanese invasion into the island just north of Australia, and provoked a complete turnaround for the Allied Forces. From that engagement, all other invasions were made by the Allies, who were now on the offensive, and would eventually come to a victorious conclusion.

I thought it was time I enlighten my fellow Americans. My next door neighbor, Vicky Kaseorg, suggested we write a factual chronicle of my experiences, the snippets I remembered. She has done a great job of editing and I will always love her for her suggestion.

Milne Bay was absolutely the most important battle of our times. Had Milne Bay been lost, this whole universe would not have been the same. That is one man's belief...mine. And I was there. I ought to know.

Turning Points * Vicky Kaseorg

Table of Contents

Milne Bay, New Guinea 1942	11
Chapter One: Becoming a Soldier	32
Chapter Two: A Formidable Figure	62
Chapter Three: Battles	83
Chapter Four: The Turning Point	104
Chapter Five: After the Battle	122
Chapter Six: Back In the States	146
Chapter Seven: Malaria	166
Chapter Eight: A Revelation	173

MILNE BAY, NEW GUINEA
1942

The great battles of WWII, those game changing decisive skirmishes, were fought in romanticized places with exotic names- Pearl Harbor, Midway, Guadalcanal, Stalingrad, Tripoli, Normandy. No one has heard of Milne Bay. And yet, the battle of Milne Bay was the first time the ferocious and invincible Japanese were turned back by ground forces. Had Milne Bay fallen to the Japanese, Australia might have toppled, or at least, been cut off from the Allied forces. With two years yet to go before the Manhattan project reached completion, this might well have changed the outcome of the war. History may have forgotten Milne Bay, but the Japanese and the Allied troops based in Southeast Asia knew that it was pivotal.

I, however, had never heard of it, and never would have heard of it had the elderly gentleman not moved in next door to me. I cannot say that I eagerly sought his company, or yearned to hear his WWII stories. I would like to say I had, because it would paint me in a much more favorable light than reality does. Instead, it took me a few years of hearing bits and pieces of the war stories before I realized my neighbor Comer Hawkins had something worth saying, and it behooved me to listen. Still, I didn't listen, really listen, until Comer and his wife Evelyn ended up in an assisted living center, trapped in a place neither wanted to be, but knowing it was the best of many unpleasant alternatives.

When Evelyn was diagnosed with Alzheimers, Comer began to fight a new war, and one that he knew would not end in victory. The best he could do was not surrender without a fight. Watching his courage facing this truly insurmountable foe, I wanted to hear about this strange place no one had ever heard of, the place where Comer served during WWII and developed the strength to take on this final battle. When I told Comer I wanted to write his story about what happened at Milne Bay, his eyes glistened.

Milne Bay is at the center of a horseshoe shaped inlet on the east coast of New Guinea. It is a deep bay with water that drops so suddenly off shore that a 5,000 ton boat can dock just 40 feet from the shoreline. The beach itself gives way almost immediately to impenetrable jungle. While from afar it looks idyllic, primeval, innocent, and beautiful, the soldiers who were stationed there while enemy pilots circled like buzzards overhead, described it as a horrible place- a swampy, boggy, wet, malaria infested, hell hole. My guess is it was not on their top ten vacation destinations list even when there was *no* war going on.

On the tip of the Papuan mainland, a small Allied base was carved out of the jungle, and given the density of this arboreal paradise, carved chip by laborious chip. General MacArthur knew that Milne Bay would be invaluable in protecting important sea lanes to Australia and Port Moresby, though he had little faith or respect for the Australian soldiers in protecting the base. MacArthur felt the Australians were ill prepared, wouldn't fight when the formidable enemy appeared. The mistrust was mutual. The Australians were not enamored with MacArthur either, especially when they arrived at this fetid, swampy, snake infested base that was to be home for the next few years.

A battalion of U.S. soldiers were sent to Milne Bay as punishment for racial atrocities by one small group of them during training in the nearby Australian city of Brisbane. Among that battalion was the 104 battery of 200 soldiers from a small town in Alabama. Many of the 104 were assigned to antiaircraft support for the Australian troops who would be deployed should the Japanese attempt to take Milne Bay. Corporal Comer Hawkins, was assigned as the leader of the first gunner crew, and his twin brother Bill, leader of the third gunner crew. They would be among the first to engage the Japanese fighter pilots. They had not been separated since the beginning of the war, and now within sight of each other in their gun pits, they crouched as the air raid warnings blared notice of yet another incoming attack. Comer was my friend, my old neighbor, but I wouldn't meet him for another 58 years. Given the conditions he would endure for the next four years, it was remarkable I was given the opportunity to meet him at all. The fact that Comer lived to become an old man was evidence of the strength of character that was being further refined in the furnace of Milne Bay.

An airfield in Milne Bay was considered critical. It would allow Allied planes to operate in the South Pacific and protect Australia. There was an airfield at Port Moresby on the southern shore of the island, but it was separated from the flight path to south Pacific targets by a precipitously towering obstacle. Pilots were forced to fly over those imposing Owen Stanley Mountains, severely reducing their target range. An airstrip at Milne Bay was crucial.

Battery 104 landed with the rest of the battalion and began digging through the thick coconut groves to develop an airstrip. The Mangrove and coconut trees were so solid, so entrenched, that the troops quickly learned that the only way to clear them was with dynamite and bulldozers. Saws and axes were ineffectual. To add to this cheery task of blasting thick impregnable coconut trunks, the troops were flooded with monsoon precipitation while whacking ineffectually at the trees. The average rainfall was 200 inches a year. Though the actual rainy season was short, those few weeks were a torrential onslaught. The rest of the year was unbearably hot and humid. Jungle plants thrived, as did deadly snakes, and rancid standing pools of water that bred mosquitoes carrying their own personal warfare. Malaria and yellow fever at times felled more soldiers than the air raids, along with dysentery and typhus. Club Med steered clear of Milne Bay.

Turning Points * Vicky Kaseorg

The Gili Gili Plantation was already semi-cleared from the jungle and chosen for the Milne Bay airstrip site. There were some elementary roads in place, and a few buildings and sheds. Natives of the area, the aborigines of Papua New Guinea were perpetually cheerful and helpful. One of the great mysteries of the war is *how* they could be so cheerful in such a place. They helped first to unload the cargo ships, moored in the deep bay and tied to shoreline coconut trees. Then the supplies were carried to the airstrip site. American engineers performed veritable miracles, assembling a functional airstrip in just three weeks.

Meanwhile, the young handsome first gunner commander, Comer Hawkins, and his crew, along with the rest of battery 104, began building gun pits for their Bofor antiaircraft guns. The pestilent stink of rotting vegetation surrounded them as their army boots sank into the dank morass. Sweat poured from their bodies. Their muscles throbbed as they strained against embedded stumps, chopped iron hard logs to usable sizes, and swatted at the ever present mosquitoes. The fresh breeze off the ocean was all that made it bearable.

To build the airstrip, the swampy ground had to be drained, the brush cut and cleared, the stumps blasted out. Gelignite, a powerful explosive was used to fell the hearty coconut trees. Some 2300 coconut trees had to be removed for the 8,000 x 300 ft airstrip. I would have loved to have seen those hearty coconut trees being blasted to smithereens with dynamite. That's one way to flake a coconut.

Native workers dug drainage ditches and emergency slit trenches all around the strip, mostly with hand shovels. Every few seconds, the shovel would clang and entangle on a thick and impossibly dense web of roots. With sweat cascading in rivers between their shoulder blades, the cheery natives chopped and tugged and groaned until the tangle broke apart and a small headway was made in the slowly expanding hole. Without the village workers, the troops at Milne Bay would have been sorely pressed to accomplish the daunting task. Sadly, it was the villagers who suffered most from the Japanese when they landed at Milne Bay in 1942.

Due to the oppressive heat and high humidity, the troops wore shorts and rolled up sleeves, when they wore anything. This contributed to the malaria problem. The mosquitoes had all the more skin exposed for their deadly buffet. It may also have contributed to the preponderance of lovely ladies swarming throughout Comer's war tales. Comer, with or without his sleeves rolled up, was apparently irresistible to mosquitoes and to pretty girls. War is hell, but Comer with his lust for life, was not going to let hell ruin the whole war for him.

Along with Australian gunners, the American 104 Coast Artillery Anti aircraft corps (CAA), manned the #1 airstrip at Milne Bay. Besides setting the Bofor guns strategically along the strip, dummy guns were made from coconut trees to confound the enemy. The weeks settling in were constant work, creating homes, safety trenches, latrines, gun pits, and mock gun pits. When the rains hit, the latrines overflowed and the pleasant smell of mildewing human waste melded with decaying roots and deep black swamp rot. The troops quickly learned to take shallow breaths through their mouths.

Rain and mud were perpetual enemies. The roads required unending repair. Trucks were forever sliding into the drainage ditches along the sides of the roads. Muddy potholes had to be filled with whatever was available- food cases, shell boxes and coconuts. The rain was so relentless, that at times, soldiers were up to their necks in water in the slit trenches. Their clothes grew moldy, their feet and toenails developed fungal infections. Water dripped into all the supplies, and into their tents. The waters rose to the level of the cots. The pervasive dampness mingled with their sweat in the steamy jungle. And always the buzz of the malaria laden mosquitoes hummed near their ears. They were constantly swatting at their faces, their slick sun-burned arms, and their muck encrusted legs. When they scratched at the welts left by those ubiquitous blood suckers, they left smears of black swamp mud against the reddened fingernail streaks.

The gunners and all troops went shirtless, but never removed their helmets. Not only were they ever vigilant for dropping Japanese bombs, but also, the real danger of concussive falling coconuts felled more than one soldier. (The casualty coconut rate is rarely reported which goes to show that the really interesting aspects of war elude most historians.) Their hair lay flat and soaked against their scalp.

American engineers were in charge of the road construction. There was so much work to accomplish in such a short time, that infantry were often put to work as engineers. The 104 CAA watched their compatriots unfurl an air strip out of the jungle while they steadily dug their slit trenches beside their carefully maintained Bofor gun pits. They seldom left the gun pit, always prepared for the appearance of the enemy that could swoop in overhead at any moment.

The food was primarily tinned "bully" beef or sardines, hard biscuits, powdered milk and powdered eggs. Sometimes there would be grits for the Alabama boys of the 104 CAA.

"We loved that, when we could get grits," said first gun commander, Comer Hawkins, "We were all from Luverne, Alabama. Nothing better than grits to an Alabama boy."

The resourceful Australians would fish in a unique manner. They would throw live grenades in the water. With the explosion, hordes of dead fish would float to the surface. The soldiers grabbed the fresh meat, being careful to toss back the highly poisonous Parrot fish.

"One bite of that and we would be floating along with all those other fish," Comer explained.

There were serious dangers from other animals as well. Crocodiles of prodigious proportion inundated the many swamps and streams. Dangerous barracudas prowled just offshore in the deceptively peaceful and clear, pristine waters. Comer told a rather gruesome story of an escapade after he and his gun crew beat out a path from their gun pit to the ocean. The ocean afforded soothing relief from the oppressive heat and filth, but it had its own charms to add to the full Milne Bay experience.

"I swam in the water," said Comer, "But I never went more than ten feet out."

"Why not, Comer?" I asked.

"I have a story that answers that," he said ominously,

"One morning, four or five Aussie officers came by to swim in our beach. They were very friendly. They came to my gun pit and said, 'Let's go swimming, Mate!' I told them,' Be careful, don't go so far out that you can't beat the sharks back.' Well, they went out, and one of them went swimming quite far out in the ocean. A barracuda grabbed him, and bit his foot clean off! He managed to make it back to shore and his buddies carried him back to our pit. 'I warned you!' I told him. 'Too right, Mate!' he said."

Comer chuckled. He recounted that the soldier swooned in the arms of his comrades, a crooked grin on his face as his life blood poured out of the stub left behind by the barracuda. Bits of ripped flesh waved in the ocean breeze. I don't know if he bled to death in front of Comer, or if he did that somewhere else. This was one of the less horrendous sights Comer had to view during the war, and thus explains his seemingly callous response.

While waiting for the air raids, there were, at first, long stretches of time with no attacks. Comer and his brother, poker sharks without equal, made thousands of dollars in games with fellow soldiers. They relieved the interminable waiting in other more unusual pastimes, as well.

"Sometimes we would go wild boar hunting," said Comer, "That was very dangerous. They were the meanest son of a gun on earth. But one happy memory is when we made one our pet!"

The 104 battery received a baby feral boar from the natives of Queensland. They became quite attached to the pig and raised it to adulthood.

"We named it Abo, after the aborigines," said Comer, "He was our pet. He was tame as could be. He was as big as a horse. We would get on him and ride him! We fed him our scraps. He weighed at least 500 pounds. We all loved him. Then the Japanese had blockaded the bay and were torpedoing all the supply ships. For several weeks, no food ships got through. We were starving. The Australians said they had to kill Abo so we wouldn't starve. The cook refused to kill him and we did too. The Aussies killed him anyway, on Thanksgiving in 1942, but we all refused to eat him. He was our pet!" An interesting irony- the hunted becomes the pet, the prey becomes a friend. Much later, Comer would describe enemy POWs similarly.

The first air-raid was August 4, 1942. The air strip was complete but the air raid siren was not yet functional. A Japanese Val dive bomber and four notorious Zero planes from the 5th Air Raid unit roared overhead. Before the Allies had any warning, the planes were above, barreling in a long, low strafing run to destroy the airfield.

Comer stood behind his gun crew and at the time was positioning a man on a 50 caliber machine gun. All along the strip flak was pinging, the guns were shrieking, "Ackackack!", and soldiers were diving into slit trenches. Guns exploded in cascades of kabooms as the gunners let loose their barrage. Dust exploded in a wave following the course of the menace before them.

"My job was to direct fire," Comer explained, "And so the gunner was sitting at the 50 caliber gun and I was at his back. I turned him on his swivel to face the Zero, and followed the smoke trail to know where to aim. When I had him positioned, I yelled 'FIRE!'"

The shell found its target. There was a deep rumble and then an explosion. Leaving a trail of black smoke, the plane sputtered to the ocean and then plowed into the waves. The sea violently bubbled over the metal carcass.

That was the recorded first "kill" at Milne Bay, and Comer was credited with that honor. I read about this first kill in other sources, but Comer was not specifically named.

By August 8, the air raid sirens were functional and future air raids were no longer a surprise. Radar could detect the planes from a hundred miles out, giving the gun crews 15-20 minutes to prepare. Comer was never caught unawares again.

"We were always ready," he said, "It took several men to operate each gun. We needed two gunners, a shooter, a wheelman, two men to pass the ammunition...the shot being heavy. One man would hand it to another who would hand it down the line to another. He handed it to a man standing on the platform who would drop it in the hopper. The hopper held six shells. They would all go out faster than you could say 'boom'. We had no chance of shooting them down, but we kept the airplanes high. We really had no chance of shooting down those low strafers. Never got a one with the Bofor."

Comer watched many American planes limp back after a bombing raid. He said they would frequently crash on landing and belly slide in. They would all listen to the wrenching screech of metal hitting the metal plates of the runway, and watch the planes careen wildly from one edge to the other, while sparks flashed from underneath. And then the horrible keen of the mangled plane would end and the plane would stop, the crew inexplicably intact. Of the 200 men of Comer's unit, a remarkable low casualty of only two soldiers for the entire time at Milne Bay was recorded.

"I remember those casualties," said Comer, "We got a direct hit in the slit trench and it caved in. We had to dig them out by hand. Billy Wolfe and Malvin Wilkins. Wasn't my gun crew, was the #4 gun pit, but I helped dig them out. One of them had his ear drums burst. The other had his brain shattered. He was disabled for life. Both were from my hometown of Luverne."

During the intense period of air raids, many men were felled by malaria rather than bombs. Comer had malaria, but it didn't become severe until after the battle of Milne Bay.

" I almost died," he said, " I was in a coma for three days. They tried to keep liquids down, nothing was staying down. Asked me who my next of kin was, but I told them I wasn't gonna die. I asked them to do something for me. 'Bring me cornflakes and milk.'

"I sat under a shade tree, and had a bowl, and upchucked. Then I poured me another bowl, and upchucked that too. By the third bowl, it started to stay down. I ate the whole box and that was the turning point. I cured my malaria with corn flakes."

The Japanese pilots accelerated their air raids. Meanwhile, a Japanese transport ship landed and deposited an infantry of ground troops at the northern horn of the bay. The Japanese troops pushed through the jungle, slaughtering the natives as they went. Some reports claimed 10,000 Japanese were beating their way through the jungle. The Milne Bay battalion waited nervously as exaggerated and inaccurate reports of Japanese numbers continued. They knew the Australian infantry was meeting the enemy in the jungle, but the gunfire sounded ominously closer as the week stretched on.

They could hear the deep percussive boom of the tanks, the echo of gunfire thrown back from the lofty mountains. The smell of sulphur, gun powder and smoke wafted on the still, malignant air. The distant sound of engines rising in pitch as they came near filled the skies, a fearful background hum in the cacophony of battle symphony. Meanwhile, at the airfield, the American Kitty Hawk planes continually rose to engage the enemy. Engines whined, then roared to life, lifting one after another into the clouds. When they returned it was always tense, Comer reported. Often, a lone Kamikaze pilot would try to slip into the tail end of the line of friendly aircraft.

"I remember one incident when a Kitty Hawk had returned and we saw another plane coming in from the ocean. He flew the whole two mile length of the runway, and then came back, strafing planes the whole way. We all saw him. One of the fellas went to the edge of the runway. He only had a rifle. He stood there and started shooting when the pilot was only 100 feet away. Shot the pilot in the head. The plane glided out and crashed in the ocean." The audible sizzle of the hot engine engulfed in deep cold water was quickly lost in the tumult of gun reports, screams, and explosions.

As the Japanese advanced, Comer and most of the gunners and troops were moved from airstrip #1 to Airstrip #3, to meet the imminent threat head-on.

"We knew that was where the Japanese were more likely to hit, especially when they were marching through the jungle towards us. It was a miracle that with 2000 pound bombs falling around us for all those years, we only had two injuries out of 200 men in our battery. There was not a single war death in our battery.

"We were just a bunch of country hicks...but we were patriotic and we were brave. Half of them never even finished high school. But they all sent money home to their mommas."

Those young men, some not out of their teens, slipped their paychecks inside carefully folded letters, licked envelopes closed with white lips, and addressed them to homes and mothers they might never see again.

As the Japanese pushed closer and closer to Airstrip #3, the small team of gunners and remaining troops guarding the airfield were getting nervous. They could hear the fighting grow louder, the smoke swirling out of the jungle closer, the stench of fear and gunpowder and blood overtaking the briny smell of the ocean, until Comer's commander gave the order to "fix bayonets."

The Japanese were less than half a mile away. Comer and his crew had been waiting by their gun, the massive Bofor. They couldn't see the enemy, but they could hear them. Shots rang out continually, the deeper percussive sound of the tanks firing, the shouting and cursing and screaming of the wounded and the attacking troops. Comer's gun crew had never left the antiaircraft guns the whole war, thus far. Now a commander, eyes steely grey, called to him, "Out of the pit, men, and fix bayonets. Be ready, and listen for my order to advance."

The men, dry-mouthed and pale, silently fixed their bayonets on the tip of guns they had not yet had to use. The gunners behind them were lobbying shells into the jungle right over their heads. Each time the shells slashed through the air, whistling just overhead, the men cringed. Comer objected, "They are going to fall right on us!" The officer put a hand on Comer's shoulder.

"You will be ok. They will not fall here."

Turning Points * Vicky Kaseorg

One right after another, the shells went whooshing not 30 feet above them. The air, already heavy with humidity, seemed unable to hold another thing, and the men below could feel the heat pressed and pushed down atop them with each frightening scream of shells exploding from the guns at their back. The officer's assurances did nothing to assuage Comer's fear. He knew errant shells could and often did fall short of targets. But he did not cringe, not visibly. "I must not let the men think I am afraid," he thought.

A photographer approached the men, lined up and facing the jungle with its fearsome noises and smoke and horrible screams.

"Soldier," he said to Comer, "Would you stand still for me while I take a photograph?"

Certainly! Why not! Shall we pop open some champagne and truffles while we are at it? Gentleman, excuse me, could you pause the war while I pose for posterity?

Comer nodded, without smiling, and turned towards the camera. He stood shoulder to shoulder with his gun crew, rifle against his shoulder with bayonet fixed. The photographer snapped the picture of the solemn men, with the jungle in the background, while the shouts and screams of the men fighting mingled with the screaming of the shells overhead. Comer knew he was going to die.

Comer Hawkins (right) 1942 Milne Bay
with bayonet fixed, preparing to engage the enemy

CHAPTER ONE
BECOMING A SOLDIER

"First, I'd like you to read this short story I wrote," said Comer, when I asked him to prepare for our interviews about his life as a WWII soldier.

"Is it a true story?" I asked.

"Oh yes," he said, "You can take it home if you like."

This is the story, which he felt gave a foretaste of his time as a gun crew commander fighting for the Allies against a formidable enemy.

Tangible proof

A True short story by Comer Hawkins

Turning Points * Vicky Kaseorg

In the early 1940s, an American antiaircraft gun crew was stationed in New Guinea at Milne Bay. The gun crew was comprised of a gun commander and 16 men. The gun commander was a good-looking 23-year-old man, easy-going and well liked and respected by his gun crew. He was also the toughest man on the island. The gun emplacement was the number one defending position. This was due to the position of the emplacement and also due to the fact that the gun crew was the best of the anti-aircraft battery. Up to the writing of this story, the crew had accounted for 80 downed Japanese fighter aircraft, a feat still standing as a record.

In the years of 1942 and 1943, this particular gun crew had suffered through and survived 101 high level bomber attacks. Sometimes as many as 100 medium bombers made the raid. At one given time over a period of ten days, the bomber attacks had been exceedingly heavy and of very devastating severity due to the uncanny accuracy of the pinpoint targeting.

One night, during this period after having been "red warning alerted", which meant the enemy planes were less than 100 miles away, the American gun commander was sitting at his gun emplacement and noticed a very bright flash of light on a point of the island about seven miles across the bay from his gun pit. He watched closely and saw a second and then a third flash of light. He made a mental note to remember this but by then the Japanese bombers were overhead and the bombs were falling. This was the most terrible bombing raid experienced up to that point.

The next day the American commander reported the light flash to his captain. It was immediately suspected that a guiding light for the bomber was being employed. The American gun emplacement was supporting an Australian fighter plane group so the captain asked the Australian Wing Commander to send one of his pilots to fly a low-level reconnaissance to see if he could detect any unusual activity or any evidence of the light. He reported back that he could not.

The American gun commander, not being satisfied with the report as he knew for certain he had seen the flashes, sent word to an Australian infantry captain who was a friend of his to come to see him. The Australian captain came posthaste. The American told his Australian friend the circumstances and of his suspicions. The captain asked his American friend what he would like him to do. The American told him he would like him to send two of his best men to make a foot reconnaissance and to see close up if there was any criminal activity in evidence. The Australian said he would have his man there by mid afternoon. This he did and the American explained to the Aussie soldiers what he wanted them to do and showed them through his telescopic gun sites where he thought the light might be approximately coming from.

Before the Aussies left for their trek through the jungle, the American told them to bring back some tangible proof or evidence that a flasher was there and active.

The next morning the Aussie soldiers were at the American gun pit bright and early. The American of course asked if they found anything and if they had any proof or evidence. One of the soldiers handed the American a wallaby drawstring tobacco pouch which was popular with the Australian soldiers. The American drew the strings open to see the contents of the pouch as it was evident it contained some object. He upended the pouch into the palm of his hand. It was two human ears.

I gulped. This was not the man that I knew. I could not imagine Comer ordering the dismemberment of the enemy, no matter how vile they were. This was the kindly gentleman who walked slowly on my street before ending up in this Nursing Home, meeting and greeting everyone in the whole neighborhood by name. He was gentle and soft voiced, a smile and an encouraging optimistic word always on his lips. I just could not see Comer slicing off someone's ear or ordering someone else to do so.

Comer had been anxiously waiting for me, with his notes balanced on his lap when I came for our first official interview. I had called first to offer to take him and Evelyn to lunch. Comer, now 93 years old, lived on the second floor of the assisted living center. Evelyn, afflicted with Alzheimer's, lived a floor below him in the "memory care" unit. When Evelyn was diagnosed with Alzheimers, and Comer's own health began to fail, I became the person I should have been for the twelve years they were my neighbors.

At first I began taking them on weekly drives, mostly out of pity. Gradually, as I came to know them, the pity gave way to genuine respect, affection, and friendship, and finally admiration.

On our weekly jaunts, we would stop at favorite fast food restaurants, then with the food balanced on our laps, drive around and enjoy the scenery. It was on these drives that I learned of Comer's exploits as a WWII veteran in the South Pacific theater of Milne Bay.

"Where?" I had asked him.

"Milne Bay."

"Where is Milne Bay? I never heard of it," I admitted.

"No one has," he lamented, "But do you know it was the turning point of the war?"

That sounded a little farfetched to me. I thought Midway was considered the turning point in our fight with the Japanese, but I have never claimed to be a war expert. He began to tell me stories of Milne Bay, and I realized Comer was right. Milne Bay *was* a turning point. It might not be the *only* turning point, maybe not even the most important turning point, but it *had* played a crucial role in WWII and no one has even heard of it! I decided this 93 year old man needed to tell his story, and needed to tell it soon.

The week after I asked Comer if he would agree to let me write my next book about his experiences, I called to see if he and Evelyn would be ready for our usual lunch in the car.

"I just got out of the hospital," he explained, "I don't think I feel up to lunch."

"The hospital! What happened!"

"Well I seem to have a clot in my hip. And so they tried to bust it up but nothing worked so far. They put me on medicine. It will eventually dissolve, or move into my heart and kill me."

"Are you sure you feel up to an interview?"

"I'm just sitting here," he said, "I would love to interview if you feel you can take the time." That was when he handed me the short story. When I finished it, I asked, a bit tremulously, "Did you order the ears cut off of the enemy?" unconsciously putting my hands over my own ears.

"No. That was the scouting party's idea." (I breathed a sigh of relief and lowered my hands) "All I wanted was tangible proof. It was an Australian, a traitor. He was guiding the Japanese in. He was causing the death of our troops!"

"I guess you had to stop him."

"Yes," said Comer. I presume they killed the traitor before cutting off his ears, but I couldn't bear to ask.

"Well then, let's get right to it. Do you mind if I tape record you?"

"No, you better, so you don't miss the details." He sat up, and looked expectantly at the tape recorder then began in a voice he could have used on the radio, "Now this is the story of a young soldier at Milne Bay." (I smiled as I remembered his short story where he described himself as a young handsome soldier.)

"Can you tell me a little about the background...how you enlisted, how you got to Milne Bay?" I asked.

Comer paused briefly, glancing at the tape recorder, "A question has been asked about how I came to be in Milne Bay. I will now proceed to tell you...."

Comer Hawkins was born in the small, poor town of Luverne, Alabama, population 6,000. On March 11, 1919, Comer and his twin brother, Bill, entered the world, joining his four year old sister to round out the family. His sister always told him that he was the first twin that popped out. She may well have known. Comer was born at home, though an old friend, Dr. Foster, came to his house to assist in the delivery. His mother was known by everyone in the town as Miss Susie.

"My mom stayed at home, like most women back then, and she was a great cook. Everyone revered her. Everybody kowtowed to Miss Susie. She was soft spoken, dear and sweet, but she had a forceful demeanor. No one crossed Miss Susie."

(I wondered if Miss Susie would have ordered ears cut off of a traitor...)

"My dad was a country gentleman. He had a pork pie hat, and you would have called him a 'dandy'. He was a landowner. We were land rich, but we didn't have money. He had several tenant farmers on his 50 acres. We were cotton and peanut farmers, like many of the farmers of that day. Well, the boll weevil came in 1929 and wiped out our whole crop. I think a lot of folks don't know this but you know what caused the Great Depression? The Boll Weevil!"

(Again, just like the under-reported wartime coconut casualty rate, how many history books ever mention the Boll Weevil as the cause of the Depression?)

"Everyone was mortgaged to the hilt! My Daddy wouldn't let his sharecroppers starve, though. He took care of five families and our own family. We never went hungry, but we went broke. He died shortly after that. I think all that hardship killed him. Now we still had our house and the five sharecropper houses. We rented those out, and the house was already paid off. My mom lived a frugal life and we made do.

"Back then, there weren't many expenses. There was no electricity, no one in our town had that yet. We used oil lamps till I was a teen. There was no indoor plumbing, no sewage system, no telephones. When I was older we got those phones that you had to crank. Do you remember those?"

Of course I didn't remember them personally. I was too young, but I had seen pictures of them. I realized as Comer recounted his childhood, that he was a walking, breathing history lesson. Why had I wasted those twelve years when he was my neighbor not having him teach my home-schooled daughter about life in the early 1900s? He was certainly more interesting than a text book, and cheaper too.

"My daddy had a beautiful horse and buggy, and the doctor and postman had a Model T Ford, but no one else in the whole town had cars or buggies.

"Things began to pick up in 1935. Like I said, my mama was frugal and rented out the houses and we still had a small farm. Our first car was a 1936 Ford, paid

$170 for it. That was a lot of money back then. By then, lots of folks had cars. I went to a big school house and graduated in 1937. I was a very good student...well, until I got into football and girls. Up till the 9th grade I was exempted from finals cause I was so good in school. But I was good at football too. We won the varsity championship in 12th grade, but I was too little to play Varsity until that year."

"Really!" I said, surprised, "Aren't you around six feet tall?"

"No," laughed Comer, "Barely 5'9, but that might a helped me. I was scrappy and always having to defend myself. I got tough because I was little."

"What did you do after you graduated from high school? Did you go to college?"

"No, I worked for the state highway department. Jobs were still hard to find, but the doctor and a state legislator who was a family friend helped get it for me. I tried out for a football scholarship at Mississippi State. But I didn't get it. I was too small. So for three years I worked at the state highway department. I was an engineering aide.

"I worked there till 1940, and then the draft came my way. I had a draft number, and knew I would be drafted, so my brother and I decided that instead of being drafted, we would just join the National Guard. That way we would always be together with the other boys from Luverne. If we'd been drafted, we'd be sent all over and separated. By joining the National Guard, my whole battery ended up being my friends from Luverne. It was a small town, and all of us in the battery knew each other from home!

"Now at that time, joining the reserves was the same as joining the army. My brother Bill and I were both sent to Camp Stewart in Georgia for training. We trained for just a few months, February to December, and well, you know what happened in December, 1941. Pearl Harbor was attacked and they cut our training short. We were sent immediately to New Jersey where we were supposed to get on the Queen Elisabeth. While we were getting ready to be deployed, the QE was totally destroyed by saboteurs. So we were transferred to the Queen Mary. We were on the seas for 42 days, sent to Australia.

"Wouldn't you know it, but the saboteurs got to Queen Mary too. They set it on fire and it burned the promenade deck while we were thousands of miles out on the ocean."

No one enjoys smelling smoke and hearing the cackling of flames engulfing their walls, but thousands of miles from the nearest fire truck, it is even less enticing. Black smoke rose in giant spumes to the sky, announcing their damaged presence to any enemy pilot that might be prowling nearby. Bedlam and chaos erupted as crewman raced to douse the spiring flames. Buckets after bucket of water were splashed onto the conflagration. The acrid smell of burning creosote mingled with seawater, as the hiss of steam erupted when each dousing bucketful was plashed against the blackened wall.

"While we were fighting that fire, the ship radio comes on and it was President Roosevelt. He was saying, 'Now hear this, the nation is mourning the loss at sea of thousands of American troops on the Queen Mary, burned at sea.' That was *us* he was talking about!"

"Didn't he know?" I asked.

"Oh yes! He was saying that to throw the submarines off guard. The German U-boats were all over those waters. We had thirty sub attacks in those 45 days! We didn't have an anti-submarine escort because the Queen Mary was so fast. We dodged the torpedoes by zigzagging all the way to Australia. Most of the attacks were in the Indian Ocean."

"Did you see them?"

"Not the submarines, but we saw the wakes of the torpedoes go right by. There were portholes on the rails and decks, and at night they would be completely covered so it was dark and the enemy wouldn't spot us. I was Sergeant of the Guard and one night, one recruit came running up to me. He was a brand new recruit and he said, 'Sgt., there is a man at the port hole and he is flashing a light out of it.' Well, I knew right away he was signaling the enemy. 'Throw him overboard!' I yelled to the recruit. And he did."

Comer paused and looked at me. I am sure I looked horrified, though I tried to disguise it by pushing my eyeballs forcibly back in my orbital cavities.

"What happened to him?" I squeaked, then cleared my throat, and cracked my neck which was developing a crick. Just in case, I covered my ears, remembering Comer's short story about the spy flashing signals to incoming Japanese airplanes.

"Well," smiled Comer, "Thousands of miles out to sea, middle of the night...what do you think?"

I blinked, wide-eyed.

"I was kidding when I said to throw him overboard, though I probably did him a favor. He would have been shot if he hadn't drowned. He'd been signaling subs. Would have drowned all of us. But I didn't really mean for the recruit to toss him overboard...."

"He was a traitor then?"

"Oh sure. And the punishment for that is death."

Consider the options: face a firing squad and *then* be fed to the sharks, or be fed to the sharks first, while still pumping fresh oxygenated blood? Neither option was pleasant but did Comer really do the traitor a favor by sending him as a living sacrifice to the hungry carnivores of the sea?

"Another time," continued Comer, unaware of the tumult in my head, "I was on a back deck sunning and a soldier was horsing around at the stern. He fell overboard. I saw it and went running to the captain, but he couldn't stop for one man in submarine territory. Our lives depended on moving and zigzagging to outmaneuver the subs. We would've been sitting ducks...we couldn't jeopardize the ship for one man."

Comer looked down and his eyes misted, "I can still picture him flailing in that water." I was touched by the depth of his sadness seventy years later. He had chuckled over the traitor's similar demise, but the death of a fellow patriot still brought him to tears. How ironic that both the traitor and the patriot possibly ended up in the same undiscriminating belly. Sharks, like war, are equal opportunity killers.

"War is never justified...except maybe to stop mass murderers, like Hitler," said Comer, "But you know, I was young. I didn't worry about war. I thought it would be grand." He shook his head. It was clearly not as grand as he had once hoped it would be.

"The British Navy served our food aboard the ship. It was awful, and then it spoiled. For days they were serving spoiled mutton. Awful terrible. We couldn't eat it."

Spoiled mutton tastes a little like bat guano. This is considered a delicacy in certain countries where starvation is the national sport. Otherwise, most *civilized* countries feed their soldiers food that won't poison them. Comer, being from one of *those* countries, wasn't going to take this abuse.

"They served us some gelatin type dessert, but other than that, we had almost nothing to eat. We were starving. Then I noticed that the ship crew was eating good food! They had ham and eggs, good stuff! When I saw that, I grabbed some men and some loaded rifles. We went to the galley and told that crew, 'We're here to eat with you.'

'You can't do that,' the crew told us, but we said, 'Oh yes we can!' and we pointed the rifles at them."

"Did they give you decent food then?" I asked, chuckling at Comer's audacity. I believe the word 'audacity' was invented to describe Comer during his war years.

"You bet they did. We kept pointing the rifles and they fed all of us. They were starving the troops while *they* were eating high on the hog! Shortly after that, we reached Rio de Janeiro, and loaded up with supplies. We had food after that.

"Then we went on to Cape Town and the Queen Mary hit such severe storms...at times she listed more than the engineers said she should be able to without going over. It was mighty rough. Those waves in the Indian Ocean were 40-50 feet high. We were blown almost completely over- way past the degree where she shoulda stayed afloat. It was a miracle- recorded in the log as impossible."

"Did you pray?" I asked.

"No," he said, "I didn't even know what prayer was back then!"

"But God seems to have been preserving you. I mean, why do *you* think the ship listed more than was known to be possible and you all didn't drown?"

"Hmmm, I don't know. We just know it happened. It was recorded in the official log as happening. God preserving me? Seems that way," agreed Comer. Comer paused to consider this and collect his thoughts.

"So then we finally reached Australia. We landed in Brisbane and stayed there while waiting for our assignment. My brother Bill was with me. He was with me for the duration of the entire war. Finally we got our assignments. I was first gun crew commander. Bill was assigned commander of third gun crew. We were to be sent to Milne Bay in New Guinea to guard the airstrip. First we had to set up guns in Brisbane, practice digging our gun pits and shooting target practice. Anyway, we were set up along the airstrip so we got to see the pilots all the time. The Australian Pilots went out early every morning in old WWI airplanes for dive bomb practice. Those airplanes were made out of bamboo! Can you imagine!? Bamboo! Little flimsy old two seaters. Anyway, some of the fellows told me I ought to go out and fly with them on a bombing practice. They said it was a lot of fun. Told me you get to see a lot of ocean. They would fly 40 miles out, drop some practice bombs, and come back. So I said, 'I believe I will.' I was friends with one pilot out there, Izzy, and so I went and asked him if I could hitch a ride on a bombing practice. He told me, 'Sure, but not today. I need to borrow a parachute for you and I don't have an extra today. Come back tomorrow and I will take you.' So I came back the next day looking for Izzy and couldn't find him. I went to some other pilots and they told me 'Izzy never came back yesterday from the bombing raid.' They never found him."

"Did they look?" (This is an example of my riveting, insightful interview style. It is why up until this point in my literary career; I have avoided thoughtful subjects like war.)

"Well of course they *looked*, but there were 40 miles of ocean to search. He could have gone down anywhere. And you know, crashing in the water is just as bad as crashing on land. The impact hitting the water will kill you."

"If you had gone with him..."

"I'd be dead too," Comer finished.

"Someone was watching over you." (I may not know war, but I know God, and His fingerprints were all over that one, in my opinion. Yes, I know what you are thinking. If God was all over this one, where was He for poor Izzy? I am a writer, not a theologian. Go ask your pastor.)

"Yes, I do believe that is true. It is a wonder we got through that war- bamboo planes...only had wooden guns when we started. We were so ill-prepared for that war. The guns would shoot only 10,000 feet , but the Japanese figured that out pretty quick and just stayed above that. They flew 300-400 mph....no way our Bofor guns could hit them. Those early Bofors were awful. We had to aim by hand cranking them. We had no chance of hitting the target. The planes were too fast. By the end of the war we had 50 calibre machine guns and those were great. We started shooting planes down then. In the end we had electronic guided Bofor guns. They were much better. No more manual cranking."

Bill and Comer Hawkins - 1942

Turning Points * Vicky Kaseorg

The Bofors on first blush seemed an exercise in futility. As the airplanes appeared overhead, the men would wildly crank the gun to the correct altitude and position, but the planes had of course by then moved on. The mens' muscles screamed in agony as they whipped the crank as fast as they could, only to sight the plane in a new position. However, despite the archaic and inaccurate shots of the old Bofor guns, they did keep the Japanese pilots high, where their bombing was inaccurate and ineffectual as well.

He smiled at me and thought about those old awful Bofor guns that couldn't shoot the planes down, "We couldn't shoot them down with the Bofors, but we did force them to stay above 10,000 feet. Made their bombing raids a whole lot less effective.

"But back to Brisbane. Sitting on that airstrip we got to watch them send planes from the Islands to be worked on, patched up, and then sent back to the front. When they got one in good condition, they would 'test hop' it to see if it was ok. Well, the fellows liked to ride along on those test hops over the mountains. My brother and I decided we would go along on a test hop one day. We went to the airstrip and asked to test hop on a U.S. army plane...not one of those Australian bamboo planes. Anyhow, we got on and took off and flew out over the mountains. We were just enjoying ourselves. It was one of those two motor transport planes. We were having a good old time when suddenly one of the motors started skipping, till it skipped right out.

"We of course started losing speed and it was getting worse. We could barely stay aloft. The pilot told us, 'We're going down. If you want to get out, I got parachutes.' 'I don't know how to put them on!' I told him. So we just hung on and the plane started losing speed as we were heading back to the airstrip, sputtering the whole way. Then a few miles out, he had to bring it down. Belly landed it- pancaked it in. We slid along the ground and came to a stop. No one was hurt. I never went back up in a plane though. That was enough for me."

I remembered Comer telling me on one of our lunch car trips that he had wanted very much to join the Air Force. He had wanted to become a pilot. But he failed the vision test, and had a heart murmur that would plague him in advancing throughout his military career. He was turned down for pilot school. Judging from his response on the little test flight, it was probably after all a providential relief that he never got to flight school. God seems to have preserved him yet again.

For a short period, he was assigned to work in U.S. Publications in a ground floor office building. Naturally he found a "pretty little girl" who was working on the floor above him, and befriended her. Often they would ride back to the base on the same tram, as they both disembarked at the same stop. The pretty girl lived at home with her parents. Comer lived across the street from her in a five man army cottage.

One morning, they both stepped off the tram and started across the street. Comer was gallantly walking the pretty girl home. No sooner had they started across when they were startled by a sound of crashing, and then a horrific boom. They swung around to see the tram engulfed in a huge ball of fire. A U.S. Air Force gasoline truck had crashed head on into the tram. Flames ascended fifty feet high. There was no doubt no one on the tram survived.

The pretty girl crumpled in Comer's arms and became hysterical. Comer brought her to her mother, and then returned to his own home. As he reported it, "I too had a reaction. My dormant Christian feelings overwhelmed me, and I wanted to thank the Lord Jesus Christ for keeping me from the Grim Reaper again by just two minutes." Shortly after that tragedy, Comer was sent on to Ipswitch.

"Most of my time in Brisbane was spent doing office work. Then they sent us from Brisbane to Ipswitch, still in Australia. It was about twenty miles away to another airstrip. For recreation, they would truck us back to Brisbane. They picked us up at midnight. We were in Ipswitch to learn how to shoot the Bofor. I was an acting sergeant the whole time, though I had corporal stripes. I could never figure out why they didn't just promote me. Then I found out that my superior had it in for me. He thought he should get respect but he didn't deserve it! I just couldn't respect him."

"Why not, Comer?" I asked. This is often the case. Those who most demand respect are those least deserving of it.

"Because he was a moron," said Comer, his voice rising a little in anger, "So he black listed me. I never did get the promotion. Anyway, on one of the Brisbane rec trips, some black soldiers cut up one of the boys.

The blacks were segregated from the other troops at that time. There was a lot of tension between them and the white soldiers. The black soldier used a knife. The captain of the outfit that got cut up was incensed, started hunting them down, beating 'em up. He broke arms, and did horrible things to innocent black men. Even killed some, brutalized many. When the commanding officer found out, he ordered the whole battalion except that black battery to New Guinea as punishment. My battery included, though we had nothing to do with it. The punishment was we were never to be relieved from our post at New Guinea until the war was over. And we never were. We got leaves, but our post duty was in Milne Bay till the war ended. It wasn't fair. We had done nothing, and that was awfully harsh punishment."

In all my reading about Milne Bay, I had not seen anything to corroborate this. I didn't doubt Comer at all, but I asked him why this incident didn't seem to be reported in the few historical articles on Milne Bay that I had found.

"I believe they were ashamed of it," he told me, "They knew they shouldn't of done that! But I'm getting ahead of myself. While we were in Brisbane, I was heading back home late after going into town. The tram that would bring us back had quit running. I was five miles from home, but started walking. Anyway, a little Ford came along, with a nice couple in it and picked me up. I told them I had some scotch back at my place and I would share. So when they dropped me off, we had a drink together. I told them, 'I bet you have a pretty daughter at home.' He was the publisher of the biggest magazine in Australia."

Australia nights are magical, warm and clear. Stars stretch endlessly across the black sky, the vast unpopulated bush hushed and peaceful. If one doesn't consider that the ten most deadly animals known to mankind live in the Australian outback, it is a land that cannot help but evoke romance. Comer took this to full advantage.

"The Australians loved the Americans," continued Comer, "They knew we were there to save their country. He brought me home to meet his daughter. We hit it off right away. She was mighty nice, and such a pretty little thing. I didn't go home except to do my duties. I ended up living with her right in his home with that pretty girl. They had no compunction about that sort of activity."

Turning Points * Vicky Kaseorg

I wasn't surprised by Comer's desire to live with the pretty little girl. I didn't *just* fall off the turnip truck. However, the father that would willingly acquiesce to or condone this arrangement disturbed me a little. And this was only the 1940s. I thought the slouch into Gomorrah didn't start till after Elvis started swinging his hips, in the 50s earliest. I was also surprised by Comer's willingness to divulge this information.

"Does your daughter know about this?" I asked, because she was surely going to read this book one day, and would know about it then.

"No, no one does," he admitted, "But I am ready to tell it."

I nodded and wondered what other kinds of lurid stories were battering his brain, longing to be released. Why did he want these stories told now? How many WWII veterans were sitting in Nursing Homes waiting for someone to ask what it was like, what they might want the world to know before they headed off to question the deity that had allowed such havoc to be wrought?

"When I went to Milne, I came back to see that pretty little girl on leave, but she wouldn't see me. I couldn't understand. Well, they knew I wasn't going to stay in Australia when the war ended, and I wasn't going to bring her home with me...so she had a little breakdown."

"You broke her heart?" I asked.

"I guess I did. She refused to see me because she didn't want her heart broken any more. I don't blame her. I believe she wanted to see me, but the magazine publisher told me that he knew I didn't intend to stay with her, and she had almost killed herself over me. "

A *little* breakdown? A '*little* breakdown' is having an extra glass of wine at dinner, eating a gallon of coffee mocha chip ice cream all by yourself, buying high heeled designer boots, or throwing a few dishes at the wall, or at the rotten stinking rat that abandoned you. (Not that I have ever done any of those things, or condone *any* of them.) A '*little* breakdown' is *not* trying to commit suicide.

"That sounds like she fell pretty hard for you," I said, "Did you feel bad about her '*little* breakdown'?"

"She was a pretty little girl, but I knew I wasn't going to marry her. I guess I understood why they didn't want me to see her anymore." Comer looked a little sheepish, and continued. "Things were different in wartime," he explained, "All the wives had boyfriends.

It was expected while their husbands were off to war. In war, anything goes."

It does? I thought of Comer and the fidelity and love that he poured for over thirty years onto his wife, Evelyn. What had changed him, I wondered, because clearly, he had changed.

Chapter Two
A Formidable Figure

Corporal Comer Hawkins- 1942

"I wasn't going to let anyone in my gun pit," said Comer, "Even the commanding officers knew that my gun pit was my domain, and no one entered it."

"Did anyone ever challenge that?" I asked.

"Never."

"How'd you manage that?"

"With a rifle butt on the side of a head."

"You threatened superior officers?"

"If they tried to run my gun crew. *I* was in charge of my gun crew."

"So you were a tough guy," I said. I actually thought he sounded like a bit of a bully, but then again, I have never been in war, if you don't count the skirmishes with my older sister, Wendy. I would've butted her with a rifle if I'd had one. That was probably a wise call by my parents to keep all dangerous weapons out of our home. Since I didn't have a rifle, I used the best weapons I had at hand...my sharpened fingernails.

"I was mean," agreed Comer. (So was I, I thought, but *she* deserved it...)

"So, you left Brisbane and were stationed in Milne Bay?" I asked, wrenching myself away from the vision of those magnificent brawls from my youth.

Turning Points * Vicky Kaseorg

"Well, first we spent a little time in Portland Road. This was for some more training with the Bofors before heading to Milne Bay. Portland Road was twenty miles inland from the coast of north Australia. It was desolate, isolated, not even a place to live set up there. We had to build a mess hall and tent to sleep in. It was barren land, out in the bush. There wasn't even a water supply. We had to find water and rain puddles. We would use chlorination pills to purify it. Fortunately, the Aborigines who lived there had cisterns with a large water supply. They shared with us, even allowed us to shower using their water.

"Any way, my area was infested with the death adders. I think I told you the story one time of the big cats they used to hunt the death adders. Those snakes are only two feet long. The tail wiggles like a worm to attract prey. Those cats were big, almost the size of a hyena. They were a special kind of jungle cat. They weren't exactly tame, but they would lead us safely."

Comer had told me the story of the cats and the death adders on one of our luncheon outings long ago. The cats would go in front of the men when they ventured out in the brush. If the cat stopped, the men were warned to stop. The cat would then pounce and come up with a neatly massacred death adder. Comer was warned to never go anywhere in that section of the country without following the cat. He had told me that he was completely obedient to that warning. He always followed the cats. Imagine that- this dangerous, tough man tiptoeing behind kitty cats for protection!

"Our duties at Portland Road were to set up the airstrip there with Bofors, but no one ever attacked. It was really only a back up in case Australia was infiltrated. It never was. Anyway, I was given the #1 gun position around the middle of the airstrip. Brother Bill was the #2 gunner, furthest from the take off point."

What Comer never mentioned, and I had to discern with my own laser-beam intelligence was that he was #1 gunner because he was the best, the natural born leader, the one everyone recognized as the go-to gunner, the first line of defense. For all his bravado, Comer never pointed this obvious fact out to me. He was, in a strange way, both humble and proud.

"Each night, I would go to Bill's gun position to play poker. Since I was the one in charge, I didn't have to man the gun. So one night, I was playing later than I intended. I started home. I heard the sound of feet on that iron airstrip. We'd been warned to be careful at night...that there were still head hunters in that area. I turned around, and an aborigine was running after me. Well I took off running, shouting for my gun guard. He heard me and fired his rifle and finally the aborigine ran off. That gun guard was a good soldier but that experience with the head hunter was too much for him. He purposely shot off his trigger finger so he could be discharged. He had had enough of war.

"Lots of people did that to get out of the war. It was just too much for some people. Our mess sergeant chopped his finger off with a knife. There were some people just not cut out to be soldiers."

I was beginning to get a sense of the desperate circumstances that had forged the character of this man during that time. Comer had needed to be tough, even vicious to survive. So many softer men had not. When someone felt the lesser of two awful choices was to shoot off his finger...well that suggested that neither choice was making anyone do handsprings with delight.

"Another time I went back to play poker and again, forgot to bring my rifle and *again*, ended up coming home too late. I heard wild dogs yipping, and I turned around to see a whole pack of dingoes come out of the bush after me. Again I started running and shouting. This time the soldier on guard fired into the pack and they finally turned and ran. They came to within 50 feet of us."

"Did you remember to take your gun after that?" I asked, laughing. I own a dog, an American Dingo. Comer always seemed nervous around her, back in the days when he was my neighbor. Now I knew why.

"Yes, you bet I did! I never left my rifle behind after that," he said, "Another time, still while we were at Portland Road, the air-force sent a US army pilot with a P51 airplane to check out the runway. The pilot decided to spend the night with us. He was a nice fellow, and we enjoyed getting to know him. After chow, he took off in his plane. He was impressed by us and wanted to 'salute' us with the plane, show us what a good job we were doing. So he made two or three fifty foot high level passes down the runway. In the third pass, at the beginning of the runway, his plane started sputtering. Coasted in but it sputtered completely out. He lost power and then the airplane began a sharp descent and then nose-dived straight into the ground. The plane stuck like an arrow, tail up in the air. We rushed over to the downed plane, and we could see the pilot was seriously hurt. His forehead was crushed. We were all just heartsick. Lots of fellows used to do that 'victory salute.' "

Not much of a victory that time. Too bad. If he had been afforded a 'next time', he would likely have just given them a high five.

"It wasn't all work and sadness though. We used to look for wild pigs to shoot for recreation."

Shooting wild pigs for recreation? Whatever happened to ping-pong, or a rousing game of *Go Fish*? I had once read that one of the meanest and most dangerous varmints on earth is the wild pig.

"Comer, that doesn't sound very relaxing..."

"Oh no, it wasn't much in the way of relaxation, but it was exciting." *(unlike being an antiaircraft gunner in the Japanese sights during WWII).*

"We would go out in the bush. It was very dangerous. Once I went out boar hunting and we got out into the hills, and we saw an aborigine family- a man, wife and his little baby. They were all little. Even the man was not more than five feet tall. They were so happy to see us, all smiles. I showed him my rifle and said, 'Looking for pigs.' He said, 'Ah pigs!' and pointed to the hills. I had a chocolate bar in my pocket and I gave it to his little wife. She fed it to the baby. They were all smacking lips, having the best time eating that chocolate. Then as we walked a few feet on our way, he called out in a British accent, 'I say, old chap, shooting pig is such jolly fun!' It was so amusing to hear him say that, that little aborigine, big bushy hair, with a British accent.

"We did find the pig. A big one. I told my men to flank me and protect me when that pig headed for me. He charged at us and they started shooting. He was maybe 150 feet away, then 100...we knew we had hit him, but he kept coming. All three of us emptied all our rounds, eight rounds each. He finally stopped 20 feet from us and died. We went back to that aborigine family and told them where to find the pig. We knew that would feed his family for a long time.

"So we remained at Portland Road for about three or four weeks. And finally we were ordered to Milne Bay. It was a seven hundred mile trip."

"I presume by boat...across the Coral Sea?" (*No Captain Obvious, we swam, with army boots and full back packs, holding the rifles above our heads so they wouldn't get wet.*)

"Yes, though funny you should mention that...we did almost have to swim. We left Australia to go to Milne on a Liberty Ship. That was a big cargo ship. We were escorted by a small gunboat called a Dutch Corvette. The Coral Sea was crawling with subs. We were attacked and hit by a torpedo. It split the seam of the ship. We started taking on water but were only three miles out from Milne. We were actually preparing to swim, even put on our life vests.

"I told my brother Bill to stay an arm's length away. I wasn't gonna lose him! But we didn't have to swim. as it turns out. The boat made it into Milne Bay.

"You should have seen it. We had to do everything, start from scratch. It was thick jungle, impenetrable. Milne Bay is right on the equator. It was awfully hot, 120 degrees or more! We could only work for two or three hours a day in that heat. The jungle was just a mass of solid trees and plants. You couldn't even walk through it, it was so thick. The engineers had cleared some out for the airstrip, but we had to clear out more to put up our four tents. I had a crew of sixteen men. Then we had to cut down logs to build the so-called fort to set the Bofor in. The logs were fortifications to protect us from the Japanese raids. And we needed protection! Do you know that those Japanese had funerals before leaving on bombing runs? They knew they weren't coming back. They would be disgraced to be seen alive again. They would crash planes on us on purpose."

"*That* is as silly as wild boar hunting and even deadlier. What is the use of glory if you aren't around to witness the results?" I wondered.

"They did whatever it took to inflict damage. We taught them to stay above our guns," continued Comer, "They didn't care about our guns, per se. They cared about the airstrip. They just wanted to destroy the strip. I'd look up sometimes and see a hundred bombers in the air. One hundred and one times we were bombed by 2,000 pound bombs. If one of those hit the ground, you could put a car in the hole. They would fly over several targets in one raid. The South Pacific had several targets in their range.

"They would bomb mostly at night. The next day, the air strip would be destroyed. And every day, the thousand engineers stationed there would race out onto the strip and fix it. The two mile strip would be bombed to smithereens, nearly every day. It was amazing how fast they could rebuild. During the night, they were all taken away to safety. We had to stay, of course, and shoot at the planes while 2,000 pound bombs exploded 50 yards from us.

"Watching those engineers was entertainment for us. They would swarm over the airstrip like ants. They had interlocking iron sheets. They'd pull up the old battered sheets and then faster than you can imagine, lay down a new airstrip of those interlocking metal pieces. I couldn't get over how fast they were. Within hours we would have a brand new airstrip."

"Did you ever help?" I asked. It seemed to me that might be fun, like playing with a giant jigsaw puzzle. And less dangerous than wild boar hunting.

"Oh no, I couldn't leave my gun. Their job was to build. My job was to protect them. There were over a hundred bombing raids over the two years we were there."

"How did you survive all those bombings?" I wondered aloud.

"Sirens would warn us when planes were sighted on radar. That gave us thirty minutes, tops, to get in place. I would position my men on the guns. I had built a big hole covered with logs and dirt to protect us, right next to the guns. That was our slit trench. Unless a bomb fell right on top of us, we'd be safe.

"Well, we did have to worry about snakes. Now there is some controversy over the most dangerous snake in the world. Is it the asp, or the cobra, or the Black mamba? I tell you, the most dangerous snake in the world is the Brown Snake of New Guinea."

"Were they in the hole with you?" I asked, with a shudder. Bombs were bad enough, but at least bombs don't have unblinking eyes and forked tongues, and don't sinuously slither.They just blast you to smithereens and are done with it. No recurring nightmares to haunt you the rest of your life.

"The aborigines who helped us tried to keep them out of the hole itself, but they were only yards away in the jungle. Got an interesting story about that."

I wasn't sure this was a story I wanted to hear. I was already pretty sure Comer's stories would lead to insomnia and the need for potent sleep aids.

"There was a colonel who came by to inspect us, and asked if we had snakes. I told him, 'Yeh, about thirty feet away. But they're not aggressive. They're deadly poisonous, but if you don't bother them, they won't bother you.' Now I had 15-16 aboriginal workers

Comer's aboriginal friend and assistant

who kept our logs in place, our tents up, and cleared the immediate vicinity of snakes. The Colonel asked if he could see the snakes.

" 'Yessuh,' says the worker, and he starts poking around in the jungle with a stick. He scared up about thirty snakes within a minute, living not thirty feet from us. The colonel was flabbergasted.

"You know that same Colonel had the audacity to ask me if I could hit anything with my gun? Well I said, 'Yes Sir,' and then I had the shooters circle the gun and raise it. *Fire one*! The trigger is shot with the foot. It shoots a shell 10,000 feet before it explodes. Was like a fireworks display. *Fire Two*! Another one burst in the exact same position right inside the first burst. That was just shooting...I mean we weren't aiming at a specific target. Impressed the Colonel though. Then he realized how silly a display that was and asked, 'Not like shooting a plane when it is going 400 mph, is it?' 'No sir,' I told him, 'We have to be sure to shoot in front of them.' 'Shoot a target,' he asks me. So I put a shack in the crosshairs, one way out on the end of the bay that we used to use regularly for target practice. I yelled to my man, 'Shoot the shack!' "Now that impressed the Colonel, when we hit the shack. Idiot! He thought that was accurate shooting, being able to hit a shack sitting still, sitting right in our crosshairs. How'd you like to serve under an idiot like that? He was a Pentagon inspector, making sure we had what we needed to defeat the enemy. Shooting a shack sitting on the end of a bay is a whole lot different than trying to lock target on a plane moving 300 mph 20,000 feet above you. He didn't know a gun battle from a dog show."

I did. I had never observed a gun battle but I *had* observed many dog shows. There is little danger of death at dog shows.

"Why didn't he know that?" I asked.

"He was just some idiot sent from the Pentagon to be sure we were doing our job, had what we needed. Fools! We were using guns that couldn't shoot, hand cranking them, and being commanded by idiots." Comer shook his head, still speaking with anger at the memory of the imbeciles in his chain of command.

"In 1942, during the big battle," he continued, "We were being bombed out of sight. I had a friend, a pilot who flew a P38, used to eat with us, play football with us. One day he came out and said, 'Let's try something.' We had big 3" guns that could shoot 20,000 feet but they weren't accurate. We weren't going to hit any planes. So my friend told me, 'Don't shoot at all. When we get the red warning that the enemy is on the way, I am going to fly to 30,000 feet and wait for them. Don't shoot Comer, and they won't know I'm up there. I will shoot them down.' He knew the planes would fly just over 20,000 feet. So the superiors gave Bob permission to go up there and 'greet them'. And he did. He sat there on top of them; shot several down. When he came back, we all thought he was great. And he was."

The percentage of pilots shot down to their death was 25% in WWII. It is difficult to find exact numbers, but the bomber pilot was an exceedingly high risk occupation, exceeded only by submarine u-boat crews, who experienced a 75% risk of death! Why would *anyone* become a pilot or a submarine crew member? It seems that the more prudent jobs to go for were in engineering, putting together the giant air strip jig saw puzzles. Or trying to get a gig in a dog show, which, as I have previously mentioned, is a lot safer than a gun battle.

"Do you know, he was discharged the same time I was?" Comer reminisced, "His grandad told him he was gonna give him $10,000 to get the war out of his system, and then he was to go to school. So Bob and I went to Atlanta and we spent that $10,000 when we were discharged. And then he went to college, just like he promised. He became a sawmill man. Became a millionaire."

I was glad that brave pilot had survived, and then had gone on to celebrate his survival. So many pilots died, almost as many from combat as from training. It was a dangerous occupation. I had interviewed many WWII pilots, and asked them why they would take on such a risky role. They all answered similarly- they wanted to fly, and they knew that if they didn't defend their country...who would?

"What did you think you were fighting for, Comer?" I asked, following that train of thought. He answered me by telling a story.

"I was out with a pretty little girl [*I was to hear a lot about 'pretty little girls' in the course of our interviews!*] during training when I joined the army, and all of a sudden a man with an ax came running towards us like a maniac. I thought he was coming after us to axe us to death. I told that pretty little girl to run. But then the man started screaming, 'Pearl Harbor has been attacked!' Every one of us were ordered back to base, and then shortly after that, shipped off to New Jersey to be put on the Queen Mary and on our way to the South Pacific. We all figured the Japanese were headed to California next. I knew if I didn't go to fight them *there*, they were headed *here*."

"Was it very terrible during the bomb raids?" I asked. Comer had thus far told the stories of the bomb raids as though they were just part of a typical day, a picnic outing, a day in the office. I could not believe that it was as unremarkable as he seemed to portray it. Surely it was more horrific than he described.

"In 1942, a Japanese ship came up within two miles of Milne Bay. It lobbied shells on my position every three minutes. That was very rough on us," Comer remembered, "That was during the rainy season. It lasted two to three weeks, constant pouring rain. Our trenches filled with water. We had to stay in the trenches during the night while that ship was shelling us. We were up to our necks in that foul water. We would try to bail it out, but it would just fill back up. Sometime the shells would be coming right at us and we would have to duck, and we'd have to go under water. We were in that water for so long that all of us had rotten toes. Difficult time for all of us; all of us had bad feet. The ship would hide in one of the coves during the day. It took them several days to find it. Until they did, every night it would shell us in that trench filled with water. They finally found the ship and sunk it and that was happily the end of the shelling. Yes, in answer to your question. It was awful.

"I had built a little bridge to my gun position. Everyone knew that no one could come across my bridge. Like I told you, even my superiors obeyed that. One day a captain came and he knew he couldn't come across my bridge. So he ordered me to come to his jeep. Well I went, thinking, 'Oh-oh, I am in trouble now.' The Captain said, 'I didn't come to scold you but to pray for you.' And he did. He prayed that the Lord would take care of me."

"I would say the prayer worked," I said.

"I would agree," he answered, "Though at the time, I appreciated what he said, but I didn't think much about prayer. Now I pray all day long, but not back then."

"As your superior, he could have crossed your bridge, couldn't he?" I asked.

"Of course he *could* have. But I would've bashed him over the head if he had."

I liked the image of the little bridge to Comer's gun pit. It made me think of the the Three Billy Goats Gruff story. Comer was the troll and no one crossed his bridge unless they could answer the "riddles three". Except in Comer's case, it was the riddle One...and the riddle was unanswerable. Only Comer could cross the bridge. Period. No exceptions.

"You never got in trouble for disobeying your superiors?"

"Never. They knew I was a good crew leader and they didn't want to harass me. And so many of them were not fit for command. It is a wonder we won the war with those idiots in charge. For example, one day I was with the natives getting more logs from the jungle to reinforce the gun pit, and I came back to see all my men were lined up on the runway with their equipment. I went over there, furious. One of the officers was doing an inspection....on the runway! I mean, that was the *worst* place to do an inspection! Just a few weeks before there had been a similar incident and a lone Zero fighter plane strafed a whole group, caught 'em out on the field, killed many. I got so mad that I hit the sergeant with my gun butt. Knocked him down. But he never raised any complaint. He knew I was right. I was tough and mean. No one fought with me.

"During that same time period, I was sent for some bayonet training, so I could be a bayonet instructor for my crew. Well, I introduced myself to the instructor. I reached out to shake his hand and he took my arm and then flipped me through the air and over his back. I landed on my rifle. Thought I'd broken my back. He looked down at me and said, 'Let that be a lesson to you. Always be on your guard.' Then I said, 'I see your point.' I started to get up, while pulling my gun out from under me, then I swirled it around and bashed him over the head with it. 'Take your own advice,' I told him. He told me, 'That was uncalled for.' "

Comer should have been blindfolded and shot twenty times over. How on earth had he gotten away with so much insubordination so continually?

"We had several run-ins over the training. He had it in for me. I had a scabbard on my bayonet and was supposed to keep it on in our training so we wouldn't hurt each other. He told me to take the scabbard off and try to stick him. I never could get him...but he sure bruised me pretty bad. Anyway, I kept my bayonet razor sharp. You could cut paper with it. Before I left, I did slice open his shoulder in a training fight. He didn't like that, but I had had enough. Still....I shouldn't have done that," Comer admitted looking down, but then he shook his head, "I was out of line half the time I was over there!"

Only half?

CHAPTER THREE
BATTLES

"Malaria lasts seven years. It goes away and then it comes back." Comer was looking over his notes as I flipped the tape recorder on during our next interview session. Comer was telling me his stories as he remembered them. It was up to me to try to put them in order. He told me, "This is not a picture of the whole war so much as just little snippets of a soldier's life. You add the details and put them in order chronologically."

"I will do my best. When did you have malaria?"

"Well I caught it while I was in Milne Bay, but I had it seven years." Malaria was a gift that kept on giving.

"Everyone had malaria," he added, "It was a horrible illness. You cannot imagine how sick and horrible you feel. Nothing hurts as bad as malaria.

Anyway, my brother Bill ended up in the hospital while we were still in Milne Bay. I was on my way back from visiting him one day, and alongside the runway, I saw a submarine."

"Alongside the runway?" I asked, surprised, "Was it on land?"

"No, it was a mirage. It must have been. What else would it be?"

What else, indeed!

"The airstrip went straight out to the ocean. And remember it was right alongside the water, just a few yards away. Anyway, my buddy and I were coming back from the hospital, and hovering over the water, there was a complete and perfect Japanese submarine."

"*Over* the water?" I may not be a knowledgeable war historian, but I am pretty sure there were no hovercraft submarines during the 40s.

"I could see every detail. My buddy saw it too. So I called my commander and told him. At first he didn't believe me, but I insisted we knew what we had seen and he better send an airplane out there. It was just off shore, maybe three miles. So he sent the airplane to look, and they found it just where I said it would be. Of course, they bombed it. So we got rid of that sucker. He had been torpedoing our supply ships so that was good to get rid of him. "

Later, I researched the probability of what Comer saw as being a mirage. There is an optical illusion, known as Fata Morgana, in which mirages occur over the ocean. They mostly occur over polar regions, but can occur over warm water on very rare occasions. They are always so distorted that it is often impossible to make out what they are images of. Comer's vision of the submarine may have been a mirage, but it was highly unlikely, both in detail and where it occurred. It was an implausible mirage, at best. (Wikipedia) *(PS-Yes, I am aware that Wikipedia is a secondary source and usually not referenced by serious historians. However, in my defense, I am, first of all, not a serious historian. Secondly, all I wanted to know was: was it likely that what Comer saw was a mirage? Within minutes, Wikipedia convinced me that the answer to that query was: perhaps, but it was a very unlikely place, climate, latitude, and detail to have been a mirage.)*

"Another time we were coming back from the hospital," continued Comer, "And I looked up on a hillside to see a line of soldiers, Aussies, in a mess line.

They were the big gun battalion, you know, five inch guns. They were stationed inland from us. As often happened then, a lone Zero plane, a Japanese fighter plane, appeared. I could do nothing but watch as he strafed right down the middle of that chow line. Killed bunches of those soldiers. Very sad to see."

"How did he slip in past the radar with no warning?" I asked.

"After a reconnaissance flight or an invasion, Aussie and American pilots fly back in. Sometimes the Japanese lone fighters try to slip in behind them. Our radar doesn't tell us if it is friend or foe, only that planes are coming in. So we started issuing red warnings when planes were coming home too, but sometimes we missed those lone enemy planes."

"That must have been really hard to watch, all those men shot down right in front of you," I noted. While Comer spoke matter of factly about the horrors he had witnessed, I had seen him cry over a story he once told me of watching a baby who had been starving finally offered milk. I knew he had a tender heart, and could not fathom how he had endured those four awful years.

"It was heartbreaking. Being right on the strip, we saw lots of pilots die. There was one pilot, he was pretty famous, Inky Inksher. Good pilot. I knew him. He was right above my gun position one day when we watched his plane sputter out. He ejected, but he wasn't quite high enough. His parachute never billowed out, and he was killed. He hit the ground so hard that his shoes were buried in the soil. Seems to have set a sad precedent.

"Not many days later, the planes came back from another sortie, and we heard another sputtering. 'Oh-oh,' we all started shouting. Another pilot ejected, and we could see the parachute wasn't opening. 'Open, open, open!' we were shouting, but it never opened. He hit the water feet first. Now coming that hard down on the water, pilots were killed instantly, but at the moment his feet hit, a huge wave swelled up, came around him, and carried him softly down. Saved his life."

"That was pretty miraculous...what do you mean exactly that the wave rose up?"

"Just as he hit, the water seemed almost to be purposely going up, as though to catch him, and lower him down safely. Strangest thing to see," said Comer, "It seemed like a miracle to us. Of course, back then I don't know if I would have called it a miracle but we knew it was strange. And again, a few days later, we heard another red warning telling us planes were coming in. This one was a two motor light bomber. Now remember, we can't tell by radar if it was friend or foe. Of course normally, our boys would radio in to identify themselves. But this plane wasn't identifying himself. So I had my binoculars and was waiting, and watching. I had given my gunners the orders to get ready to fire.

'Steady, steady, steady,' I told them, peering through my binoculars. I was just about ready to yell, 'Shoot!', when I recognized him. Well it turns out, his radio was out. He *couldn't* identify himself.

"He landed, taxied to the end of the runway, and then jumped out of his plane, and ran all the way back down the runway to my gun position. It was almost a mile down. He jumped in my gun pit and thanked me profusely for not shooting him. And I knew I could have hit him. I also knew if he had been a foe, he would have machine gunned us. Remember those Japanese were suicide bombers. It was us...or them. That was a pretty tense moment, but I am awfully glad I held my fire."

That must have taken nerves of steel. No wonder this man was given such latitude by his superiors!

"It was the rainy season then," continued Comer, "We were inundated with water, and *miserable*. To top it off, they bombed our supply tent where our food was stored. Only one thing remained intact. For some reason, there were still dozens of gallon buckets of chocolate pudding. So for two weeks, all we ate, three times a day, was chocolate pudding."

I laughed, "And do you still like chocolate pudding?"

"Love it," he said, "Now of course we could fish some, in between the bombing raids. Some fool soldiers would fill their canteens with gelignite. That is a most powerful explosive. They would light it and throw it in the ocean, hoping it didn't explode in their hands. When it landed, it would explode in the water and the fish would boil up. The CO made us stop that though. Told us it was too dangerous. After two weeks of starving on nothing but chocolate pudding, a supply ship finally arrived. The starving time was over.

"I was a great poker player and made tens of thousands of dollars playing poker. So I always had money. One fellow told me, just after the starving time, that a crewman on the supply ship had a case of eggs. He offered to sell them to me for $100. All we'd eaten for two weeks was chocolate pudding. We had our regular supplies now, hard tack and jerky, tinned beef, but nothing nearly as enticing as eggs in months!

" 'Go get those eggs now!' I told my men, and gave them $100. They came back with 144 eggs. 'Start cooking those eggs!' I told my men, and called my brother Bill from his gun pit to come join us. I fed my 16 men, my brother and me, and we ate every egg. I ate sixteen eggs myself!"

$100 doesn't seem like much, but adjusting for inflation, $100 in 1942 would be worth $1,322.72 in today's money. That adds up to $9.19 per egg. A three egg omelet would be almost $28. Comer himself ate $147.04 worth of eggs.

"That was generous of you to share the eggs," I said, after considering the math.

"They were my men. I took care of my men. And my brother. Of course, my brother."

Every single time Comer mentioned his brother, he would shake his head a little, grow pensive and misty eyed, and pause. This twin soul of his heart had died a few years back, when Comer was still my neighbor. I remember the perpetually smiling Comer coming towards me that day with a grim and misery-laden visage.

"My twin died," he told me, and then he stifled deep wrenching sobs, "It is like a piece of myself is gone."

"You always took care of your brother?" I asked, in response to his egg story.

"*Always*," he said, "Another time, I got us all a real feast! A Salvation Army man would hitch a ride with planes coming in from Australia and he would always ask me if I needed anything. After the starving time, he came again. This time, I told him, 'Yes, go get me thanksgiving dinner with all the fixings for all my men and of course, my brother Bill.' We hadn't had real food but for those eggs in two years by then. So he did- I gave him $100 and he came back with turkey, gravy, mashed potatoes, stuffing, cranberry sauce...everything! A complete thanksgiving dinner for all my men, and me and Bill."

"Two years with nothing but tinned food?" I asked. Given this new information, perhaps Thanksgiving dinner at the adjusted rate of $1322.72 for sixteen men was a bargain! Undoubtedly, his men polished his poker chips in between diving underwater to avoid the

2,000 pound bombs. I would've made sure my sugar daddy kept winning.

"That fool Commander General kept the whole battalion there for four years. No reprieve. He should have been court martialed. A thousand men punished for the actions of fifty. We were on combat duty for four years. No one else in that war saw four straight years of combat duty. In fact, it drove some men plumb crazy. We had a master sergeant who was an old time National Guardsman from my little town of Luverne. He decided he couldn't take any more orders. One day, he just quit. Walked out. So they caught him and put him in the hospital as a 'psycho'.

"I had to go to the hospital shortly after that, real bad with malaria. While I was there, they had a bombing raid on the hospital. The Japanese had no honor- they bombed hospital ships and hospitals both. Anyway, the bombing started and I was too sick to move. The hospital staff ran off, and left me there, bombs dropping all around me. I was a sitting duck. Well that psycho, that big sergeant, he came and found me, carried me to safety and put me under a big tree where they couldn't see me from the air. Saved my life. I could hear shrapnel in the tree branches. Then he went off to find the doctor and staff members that had left me. He beat them up good. The next day, that staff dug slit trenches for all the patients, in case a raid like that ever happened again."

"Did they ever charge the sergeant with assault?"

"No, they did everything he asked after that. They knew they had been wrong. He was an old buddy of mine from Alabama."

It sounded like Alabama men, at least back then, didn't take any guff from anyone. *Note: never cross an Alabaman.*

"What happened to him after that?" I asked.

"He was sent to Australia, and that's where he served the rest of his term. Then he returned to the US, and had a successful career."

"The raids were very bad in late '42, right? Is that the time period you are talking about now?"

"Yes, for about three weeks, we had that awful battle. That was the turning point. Those red warning sirens were going off constantly. I had 15-16 aborigines that worked for us. All of a sudden, they would just run off....and then a few minutes later, the red warning would sound. We never knew how they did that, how they knew those planes, a half hour away, were coming in even before the radar did.

"During the bad attack, that last assault, it was three weeks of constant bombing, constant rain...it was a terrible time. They moved us from airstrip one to airstrip three. The Japanese were making their way through the jungle towards airstrip three. We were certain we would not survive. No one had ever fought the Japanese on land and won.

"The Australians saved the day. They couldn't wait to fight. They were expert bayonet fighters, best in the world. I can't say enough about them. I wouldn't be here today if it weren't for the Australian infantry. As the Japanese advanced toward our position, they were using tanks. They had a strange reflected lighting system so that the boys were having trouble shooting the lights off the tanks. It was very bad because the enemy could see *them*, but *they* couldn't see past those crazy lights to take out the tanks. They finally figured out to throw gas bombs inside the tanks. Then they started to rout the enemy. By the way, I told them to do that, when they would come back complaining about the tanks. I told them, 'Throw those gas bombs inside the tank!' A horrible way to die...but it was my suggestion."

I wondered if Comer really was the first to suggest that. If he was, he was more of a hero at Milne Bay than he had already proven to be. The tanks were the terrifying strength for the Japanese in their jungle assault. When the gas bombs disabled the men in the tanks, the tanks rolled into the muddy ditches and were swiftly sucked to inky depths while the smell of rotten eggs and diesel perfumed the air. When the tanks stopped coming, the Aussies with their bayonets swarmed after the Japanese.

"While they were after the Japanese, my job was to go in during the battle with a truck assigned to us to pick up the wounded. I had to go right into firing distance of those deadly tanks. Still, every single truck I sent in came back safely.

"How did you manage that?" I asked.

He paused and considered this, "I don't know, but I never lost a one.

"During the advance, we were feeling pretty worried. At one point, we were given a crazy command. It is a wonder they didn't send me to the stockade for life. Half my commanders were idiots, and I just *had* to keep telling them so. Where we were, just a mile or so back of us in the jungle were high mountains, 7,000 foot mountains. Do you know our fool commanders told us we needed to pack up our supplies- a rifle, a few k rations, extra socks, a shirt in our pack sack, and go 150 miles or so over 7,000 foot mountains through impenetrable jungle to retreat? Imagine that. I told them, 'No way. I refuse. It would take a month if we could do it at all and we will run out of food, for one thing...' This was to be our escape route. I told my men, 'If they tell you to evacuate, you refuse.' Fortunately, the commanders figured out it was a stupid order."

"They never tried to punish you for refusing an order?"

"What were they going to do? They knew they were wrong. Milne Bay was reported to have the densest jungle in the world. I have no idea how the aborigines managed to navigate through it. There was no way we were going to be able to make it through that jungle. Those commanders were idiots and I told them so."

"So what happened? I know the Japanese were almost on you and they really wanted that airstrip!" I knew that because I had been reading many articles about the Milne Bay attack. Everything Comer was telling me was corroborated by what I had read. Many pilots were mentioned by name, but the gunners were never identified. I had read about the incident of the first recorded "kill" when the first Japanese plane was shot down, but Comer was never given credit in the article. His description of the episode was more detailed than what I had read, but clearly describing the same incident. I knew that the Japanese were desperate to take Airstrip #3, and with the advantage of their tanks, were now perilously close to doing so. I was so glad that Comer had had that magnificent supper of thousand dollar eggs to fortify him.

"I told you how we were finally told to fix bayonets. The enemy was not a half mile away and they were coming. The guns behind us were shelling into the jungle and we were standing there, putting on our bayonets, and waiting while the shells whizzed overhead. But they never broke out of the jungle. I owe my life to the Australian soldiers. They turned them around and then gave chase. "

"So you never had to go after them with your bayonets. You stayed with your guns?"

"That's right. The Aussies chased them, fought them and killed or captured every one of the Japanese. I think maybe a few got back on a submarine waiting for them, but not many. It was awful what they did to the aborigines, though, while they were marching through the jungle. Whole villages killed, mothers, babies. Horrible atrocities.

"We were sent on a reconnaissance mission after the worst of the fighting had ended. They suspected that there were still some kamikazes lurking, so we were sent to look for survivors and stragglers. We would go out in the morning and walk half a day, and then come back.

"On one of those trips, I ran into a group of engineers. They had a camp bonfire going. A major was with them. They had potatoes cooking. I had three or four men with me, and they dived into those potatoes. Well the major pulled out an automatic 45, and ordered me to stop my men from eating those potatoes. I had my machine gun with me, and I pointed it at him, and I told him, 'Major, you go ahead and shoot, but mine will shoot faster than yours.' 'In that case,' he told my boys, 'You go ahead and help yourselves.' I had some fish we had caught and I held them up and offered my fish for the meal. We both had our guns pointing at each other, but he lowered his first. He realized he was in error. Then I lowered mine. Afterwards, he apologized profusely. We had a good time eating those potatoes and fish with the engineers and major in the end."

"Did you end up finding Japanese stragglers?"

"Yes, not that day, but when we were at our tents one day, a replacement sent from NY was on guard duty. He came and told me, 'There's a man trying to tear up your gun!' I said, 'Shoot him!' It was a Japanese straggler trying to dismantle my gun! He jumped out and ran. The moon was quite bright. We could see he was wearing a breech clout, so we knew he was a kamikaze pilot that had bailed out. He was trying to carry out his glorified suicide mission. The guard shot him. So he got his wish.

"A few days later, one of the other fellows saw another straggler. He ran down into a ditch and escaped. Shortly after that, a chaplain was using the latrine, and the straggler came out and clubbed him to death. I knew the Japanese straggler was coming back. So another guy said, 'Dig a hole and bury me in the pig path. Cover me with palm fronds. He'll be coming back on the path.' Sure enough, the Japanese straggler came, fell in the hole, and the soldier shot him. The stragglers knew they would be killed. Kamikaze pilots knew they would not be returning to Japan, so they wanted to cause as much damage as they could in the meantime."

"Were things winding down for you in Milne Bay after that?" I asked, shaking the image of the Japanese straggler yearning to take as many casualties as he could with him.

"There were no more bombing raids, so things were pretty quiet. One day, my men told me that ten or twelve new P40 fighter planes had come in and I might want to go see them. I sure did! So I walked a mile up the runway with my Aborigine bodyguard. He always carried his trusty lance with him. He would have speared his own mother for me. He was very devoted. There was a young airman guarding the plane, and he had a beautiful bone handled 38 caliber gun, in a beautiful holster. I asked him if I could buy that gun. 'Naw', he said. So I told him I would pay double whatever he had paid for the gun. 'Naw', he said. So then I drew an x in the sand, between his feet and said, 'Now you can see how well my friend can throw a lance.' And within a split second, my body guard threw that lance right on the x. The airman was terrified. 'Next time,' I said, 'I'll put the x on your belly.' So then I took the gun. Didn't pay anything for it either."

I weighed my response carefully. This was war, and Comer's toughness had saved many lives. I had come to greatly respect his devotion to his men and to his duty.

"Did you feel bad?" I asked finally. Had he perhaps told me the story with a sense of remorse over taking the gun from a fellow soldier?

"No! No! I offered him double what the gun was worth! He could have had two guns for what I would have paid him."

"But you *didn't* pay him," I reminded Comer.

"No, cause he turned me down. In war time, you can do anything. The only thing the army wouldn't abide was thieves."

I could not stop myself from proclaiming, "But Comer, you *stole* the gun."

"I didn't steal it!" he insisted, "Stealing is when you take something without someone knowing it. I offered him money. He refused."

Comer laughed remembering that story.

"But I have another sad story," he said, "I used to go in the evening to where the American Pilots parked their planes. I went to chat with a young pilot who was gong on a bombing raid to Rabaul- that was a main Japanese outpost on Guinea. It was a favorite place for them to store their planes and disperse their troops. The Americans bombed that place incessantly. Anyway, I asked him how many raids he'd been on. 'Six,' he told me, 'I just got one more to go. After seven raids, I am retired. But I got a nervous feeling about this one. You know Comer, if it weren't so deadly it would be beautiful, climbing way up in the sky with so many Japanese guns shooting at you- it looks like Chinese fireworks!' I asked him if he would climb above all that. He said he would. So I asked if I could go with him. I knew the war was winding down for me at Milne Bay and I wanted to see that view. But he told me no, he wanted to get that last one over with and just go home!

"Well, he got shot down on that last flight. He never came back from the last raid he would have ever had to go on. That was the second flight I almost went on that I would've died."

"I understand why you would have wanted to go," I said, "I wonder what it was like to go up in those planes...to climb above the bombs?" It might have been almost peaceful if it wasn't so deadly, climbing so close to Heaven.

"Yes, he said it was beautiful, and I always wanted to go. But I am glad in the end that I didn't or I wouldn't be here now telling you about it."

CHAPTER FOUR
A TURNING POINT

With the bombing of Pearl Harbor and American entry into the war, Japan had been planning how to best isolate Australia. They knew all along it was unlikely they could conquer Australia. Their intent was to prevent the Allies, particularly Americans, from using Australia as a staging area into the Pacific. They successfully made some bombing sorties into Northern Australia, but knew that they did not have the force necessary to take the continent. Their strategy shifted to try to take Port Moresby with its airfields, a city on the southern coast of New Guinea. They hoped to thereby control the Coral Sea, and prevent the Allied forces from using Australia as a base of operations. To isolate Australia, they decided a more effective strategy would be to first take over the islands, known as the Malay barrier, north of the continent. They led several attacks against the barrier islands, then set their sights on New Guinea, and Port Moresby.

They could hardly have chosen a less hospitable place to launch an offensive. New Guinea was a lush, tropical area that was almost completely undeveloped, with vast jungles. It had been a British territory, which was later turned over to the Australians in 1901. The natives were primitive, of Melanesian origins. In fact, Papua New Guinea's name is derived from the native's frizzy hair. In Malay, Papuwa means "frizzled". The Australians called their native assistants, often invaluable as guides and workers, our "fuzzy wuzzy friends." (Milner, *U.S. Army in WWII*) Comer himself always spoke of the natives with great affection.

The island is huge- 90,540 square miles. This vast area is covered with dense vegetation, a tropical rain forest so imposing that there are places that simply cannot be navigated. The natives somehow had slashed trails, barely wider than the thickness of a single man. The torrential rainfall that could dump as much as ten inches a day on the region kept the jungle floor in a perpetual morass of tangled roots, spongy moss, and muck, and mud.

While the climate and resulting jungle were imposing obstacles for any kind of military operation, the terrain itself was even more problematic. The Owen Stanley range ascends as high as 13,000 feet, jutting straight up from Port Moresby on the southern coast. While the beach temperatures could hover over 100 degrees, in the high altitudes of the towering mountains, temperatures could be numbingly cold. The mountains run down the middle of the entire length of the island like a huge dividing wall between the Coral Sea side and the Solomon Sea side. On the northeastern beach side, the foothills slope more gently to the sea and to the settlement of Buna, but the area is covered with rotting vegetation and malarial swamps. Sluggish water drained and seeping from the mountains lies in pestilential pools near the beach. Indeed, ten times more soldiers were casualties of malaria than of bullets.

An overland crossing from Moresby to Buna is a suicidal mission. The extreme temperatures, jagged imposingly tall mountains, and impenetrable jungle make it all but impossible to traverse. There is a narrow trail called the Kokoda Track that crosses the mountains, but it is hardly sufficient for troops or equipment to navigate. Yet, The Japanese settled on an attack plan that had them doing just that- travel over the Kokoda Track from Buna to take Port Moresby. Their desire to take Port Moresby by aquatic attack in the Coral Sea was turned back, in the aftermath of devastating losses in their naval arsenal at the Battle of Midway. Thus, in June, 1942, the plan was hatched for an overland assault on Moresby, via the Kokoda Track, embarking from Buna.

Despite vehement objections to the impossibility of his demands, General MacArthur ordered the Australian forces on very short notice to transport troops and supplies to Buna for a counter offensive. Comer had told me that he and his Aussie friends had little respect for MacArthur. They felt he never equipped them properly for the tasks he ordered them to accomplish and yet, simultaneously, he did not respect their abilities.

Gen. MacArthur ordered troops to defend Kokoda Track, from the Port Moresby end. MacArthur did not understand the inhospitable conditions he was ordering the troops to endure. The Australians were poorly trained for such an assault, and initially outnumbered. As the Japanese landed and built up forces on the northeast shore, things were looking bleak for any

Australian force to show up with any strength or equipment to challenge them. A small force that reached Buna in time was insufficient to impede the Japanese as they slashed through the jungle on their overland assault. While the Japanese were headed across the Kokoda track, Comer's battle at Milne Bay was taking place.

The Australians from the Moresby side tried to turn the Japanese back on their march through the Kokoda Track, but were forced into defensive positions till the Japanese were almost in sight of Moresby. The Japanese reported seeing the lights of the city and smelling the ocean. They were almost able to touch their goal, but given the ferocious brutality and war crimes later reported from that region, it was not likely to be a *light* touch when Moresby was in their grasp.

But then, the Allies began pummeling Japan at Guadalcanal. The Japanese leaders felt they did not have the strength to fight successfully on both the New Guinea front and at Guadalcanal, and ordered the troops on Kokoda Track, just 30 miles from Moresby, to retreat. This was their second humiliation. The first had happened a few weeks earlier where Comer contributed to their defeat at Milne Bay.

Turning Points * Vicky Kaseorg

While this is not meant to be an exact or complete history of the Japanese assault on New Guinea, it does serve to set the context for the battle at Milne Bay. For further reading, there are many excellent resources including the very precise and enlightening internet document by Samuel Milner, *The US Army in WWII- Victory in Papua New Guinea.* (Milner, ibid.)

At any rate, the Japanese wanted an air base on New Guinea and had originally planned to build one at Buna, and of course, hoped to take over the airfields at Moresby. The Australian forces, including American 104 CAA, Comer's battalion, had arrived in June, right under the Japanese' noses, and had been busily constructing the airstrip and support gun pits at Milne Bay. General MacArthur wisely realized that if Guadalcanal fell to the Japanese, then Milne Bay would be in their crosshairs next. Thus, he ordered the airstrips be built at Milne Bay, on the coconut plantation of Gili Gili. Comer may not have loved MacArthur, but he certainly made the right call on what the Japanese would likely do next and his orders to prepare Milne Bay would be the right strategy in the end.

It is astonishing that for two months, despite their impressive air capabilities and many reconnaissance missions over the area, the Japanese didn't discover the airfield and fortifications being constructed at Milne Bay until July. Some authorities even claim it was August before the Milne Bay base was discerned by the enemy. When they did, they immediately changed their plans. Milne Bay was now the second center of their two pronged attack plans, and the north shoreline fields of Buna abandoned. Take Milne on the S.E. tip of New Guinea, Port Moresby on the southern shore, and the Coral Sea could be effectively closed to the Allies.

"Why didn't the Japanese know that you were there for two or three months?" I asked Comer.

"It's a mystery," he said, "I don't think history knows." I had an idea, but it wasn't one that most serious war strategists would entertain. Someone was watching over my friend. Otherwise who would catch Evelyn when she fell? Other historians have suggested it was the cloud cover.

Whatever the reason for the Japanese oversight, it gave the soldiers at Milne Bay the time they needed to construct their airstrip. It gave Comer and his gun crew the time to build their gun pits, their slit trenches, and their barracks. Had the Japanese found them sooner, before their support and defenses were in place, would

Comer have survived? While historians argue over whether Milne Bay was as pivotal a battle as the Australians claim, it was inarguably the first time that a Japanese land force was turned back by Allied Forces. It finally put an end to the idea of Japanese invincibility.

As I was reading various sources about the battle of Milne Bay, I came across an article that referenced a book written shortly after the war. This author stated that a small force of American antiaircraft gunners and American engineers positioned to defend Airstrip #3 were integral in the defense of Milne Bay when the Japanese were just about to break through the jungle. The mortar attack was so severe that not a single Japanese soldier crossed onto the air field alive. I remembered Comer describing that attack, as he stood ready with bayonet drawn while the shells hissed right over his head.

The engineers and the antiaircraft gunners...credited with a pivotal role at Airstrip #3 in defeating the Japanese? I paused upon reading that. In the book by Hugh Casey, written in 1951, *Airfield and Base Development*, the role of engineers and antiaircraft gunners in the defense of Milne Bay was lauded. Casey wrote that it was the American engineers and anti-aircraft gunners who were the first American troops to engage in ground combat in New Guinea. The engineers, Comer had told me, had always been pulled back to safety during the bombing raids. The engineers were not used in fighting, not in *destruction*. The engineers were used in building, in *construction*. And yet, at Airstrip #3 in Milne Bay, both had been needed, and both had turned out to defeat the enemy. And it also said "antiaircraft gunners". That had to be Comer, and his men. Did Comer even know that history recorded his contribution to the success at Milne Bay?

"Comer!" I said, when he answered the phone, "I have a question for you!? But first...how are you?"

"Not good," he said, "My legs are so swollen they are ready to burst."

"Oh...I am so sorry. I can call another time."

"No Sugar, talking with you helps. What did you want to know?"

"I just read an article that says the American engineers and antiaircraft gunners were pivotal in the Milne victory...at Airstrip #3. Was that you?"

"I don't know who else it could've been. We were the only Americans there."

"Then Comer, you were a bona fide hero. You and those engineers."

"Well...I don't want to take credit where credit isn't due...but we *were* the only Americans there."

"Feel better," I said, "I will call you later in the week... and I will bring the article so you can see for yourself. You are a hero, Comer."

"Well, well," he said. I could hear the smile through the phone. Comer had never thought of himself as a hero. He had just done his duty, and tried to keep his brother, his men, and himself alive. I copied the article to bring to Comer the next time I visited him. If anyone ever calls me a hero in print, I want it framed. And maybe that is why I will never be a hero.

The Milne Bay battle was a huge morale boosting victory and prevented the enemy from obtaining the airstrip they so desperately wanted in the two pronged attack on New Guinea. The overland attack on Port Moresby was to end in victory for the Allies as well, with the squeeze put on Japan by Guadalcanal.

After the victory at Milne Bay, the facilities at both Airstrip #1 and #3 were improved. The airstrips were rebuilt and modified, and the Allies now had a secure base from which to conduct operations against Rabaul and Japanese airfields in the Northern Solomons without having to cross the formidable mountains of New Guinea. As Comer had noted, the Japanese never seriously attacked Milne Bay again while he was there, at least not with ground troops. They continued to bombard the strips from the air and until Comer left New Guinea, he continued to aim his ineffectual Bofor gun at the enemy pilots, forcing them too high to cause much damage.

New Guinea had been defended and Japan's hopes of cutting Australia off from the Allied forces were squashed. Comer, with bayonet fixed, had prepared to face one of the most brutal, persistent fighters of the modern era, and survived. The antiaircraft gunners and the engineers, working together, had turned the battle of Milne Bay to the Allied's favor. There is a little bit of both to make a man, to fight a war. Bombers and builders. A time to tear down, and a time to build- and a pivot on which the fortunes of the war began to turn.

****

There are not many accounts of the Milne Bay Battle. Those who took the time to record what happened at Milne Bay seemed to agree that it was an important cog in our ultimate victory in the Pacific. I had often wondered why Midway and Guadalcanal were such important battles, such inconsequential tiny islands...why would anyone fall on the sword over such tiny places? Now I knew. The interrelated tentacles of war, how each battle affected others, was something I had never thought much about. Of course it made sense. It makes sense in war and it makes sense in society. Each of us has a role to play and if we decide we are no longer interested in our part of the theatrics, the whole production falters.

Many accounts of the lives of WWII veterans describe them as emerging largely unscathed from the experience. They did not appear to be as traumatized by war, the way that was so evident in returning Viet Nam vets, for example. Was this true? Was it true for Comer? Certainly Comer was not the same man he had been during the war. It was part of the disconnect for me during the interviews. I had a hard time picturing the man *I* knew doing the things Comer described. I did not sense any despair, remorse, or trauma from his experiences. If anything, rather than harboring ill effects from the evil of war, I think he had become a better, more stable man than the wild, intractable soldier he'd described. When had he changed? What was the turning point for him? Perhaps, as in the war itself, were there many turning points?

Throughout the interview process, Comer's current situation was a sharp contrast to the tales he relayed. *Then*, he had been iron strong and self sufficient. *Now*, he was frail, struggling just to walk across the room. He was dependent on the aides in the Home to help with many needs he had once taken care of without a moment's thought. *Then*, he had been confident, even cocky, and pummeled all opposition. *Now*, he stoically accepted his diminished ability to affect *any* outcome in his life. "I just have to accept that this is the way things are now," he told me many times. He humbly downplayed his talents and his role in the war. *Then*, he had cavalierly courted the most beautiful women of the Pacific with little thought to his impact on them emotionally. *Now*, he gave unwaveringly his full devotion to a woman who could not speak a coherent sentence of gratitude in return. *Then*, nothing mattered more than his duty to his country and to protect a squadron of men assigned to his command. *Now*, nothing mattered more than his duty to his wife, her mind slowly crumbling from the devastation of Alzheimers. *Then*, as *now*, he was in battle, but the enemy had changed. Interestingly, so had the combatant and his tactics.

I had planned to take Comer and Evelyn out for our weekly drive and lunch, which had been postponed for weeks. I saw Comer several times a week for interviews, but rarely did we go out any more. Partly, I could not give any more of my time. But also, Evelyn had banged her head in a very bad fall, and had been unable to leave the Home for some time. But just as I was preparing to leave the house one afternoon for the long awaited lunch outing, Comer called to cancel, "I just got back from the doctors and I don't feel like I could even stand up, let alone make it to your car."

"What happened?"

"They took out a whole chunk of my cheek," he said, "Skin cancer. I got 15 stitches. I thought they'd never stop scraping and cutting. I could hear them scraping clear to the bone."

Well, that description took care of my need for lunch as well.

"I am so sorry," I told him, "I'll check on you at the end of the week to see if you would be up to lunch out by then."

"I would be able to interview over the phone if you have more questions," he said hopefully, "I keep thinking there is a story I need to tell you. But I can never remember what it is. I know it is important. Maybe this time I will remember it."

I had actually finished most of the interviews for my book, but I paused.

"Are you sure you feel up to it?"

"Oh it would take my mind off the pain," he said, "I tell you though, this is the last time. If they say I have another cancer, then so be it. I will not go through this again."

I can't imagine Comer saying that *then*. *Then*, he would've busted into the hospital, wrangled the doctor's scalpel from him and with his rifle butt near, threatened that doctor heal him, *or else*. 'So be it' was not in his vocabulary *then*.

One of the most interesting things I have discovered in my extensive interviews writing my books is that people are smoldering masses of inconsistencies and conundrums. Even the people you may consider pure, have pockets of darkness. I knew that was true of me...but it always surprised me to discover it to be true of others. We are a mixed bag, we humans, and we like to hope that the face we turn to the world is a pleasant one, but we all harbor murky depths. And we all have the capacity to surprise, to change, to transform in the face of experience. I wanted very much to know what changed Comer to be the man I knew today. What was the turning point? The man *I* knew was selfless, loyal, gentle, kind, forbearing, generous, and accepting. For all the qualities I admired in the Milne Bay hero, they were a different list, though both the old and the new Comer were courageous. It would only be a partial story if I stopped here, with the end of the Milne Bay battle. The molding of a man had begun there, but its effects would continue to shape who he would become. If not the war, *something* did, because he *was* changed. The man he was *then* was not the man he was *now*.

Comer's war experiences definitely formed strong opinions of the Japanese at the time. He said they were brutal to their captured soldiers. Reports of mutilation and even cannibalism led to many war crimes inquiries and convictions. Natives were raped, and then murdered as the Japanese retreated back over the Kokoda Tract. Allied prisoners were rarely allowed to live. The Australians never left wounded or dead soldiers behind if they could help it. The Japanese shot and desecrated the corpses. Comer hated this enemy. He found them to be savage and terrifying in their brutal treatment of the natives, the wounded, and the dying. He willingly, even gleefully tried his best to annihilate them. Yet Comer told me of a time when he had the opportunity to look into the hold of a Prisoner of War ship, filled to the brim with captured Japanese. I asked him how he felt, looking on them in that miserable stinking hold, smashed together and chained.

"I felt sorry for them," he admitted, though his job in the war was to kill them, a task their brutality made him anxious to perform. How does one disassociate the enemy target from the common humanity one shares with that enemy? It has to have an effect.

As I stood up to leave after one interview, my head swimming with the images of viciousness mankind could inflict upon each other, Comer asked me, "What do you think of Jesus?"

I paused and looked at him. I sat back down. *Where did that come from? We were talking about the war.*

"What do you mean?"

"Well," said Comer, "I didn't use to pray. I didn't use to believe. Now I pray hundreds of times a day. I just wondered, why do you think God had to use Jesus?

I believe in Him, and I pray to Him, but I still don't quite see *why*."

I smiled at my old friend. In all my reading and learning about World War II, Milne Bay, and battles, I had been an onlooker with no personal knowledge or understanding. I had been the one asking all the questions. It was ironic that Comer, this wise man of so many years, would be so sincerely seeking my opinion on God.

"I think God is so incomprehensible," I said, "That we cannot begin to grasp understanding Him. I think He sent Jesus in part because as humans, we could only truly understand another human. I mean, if I had a message to send to ants, what would be the only way I could communicate with them? I'd have to send another ant."

Comer laughed, "That makes sense."

We talked about God for a long time. I don't know what sparked Comer's questions, but clearly the war memories had dredged something out of his psyche.

CHAPTER FIVE
AFTER THE BATTLE

"The worst of the fighting at Milne Bay was over, so we were sent for a two week leave to Brisbane, both my brother Bill and me. Our unit was not relieved from Milne Bay duty the entire four years, but we could still have leaves now and then. We went to Townsville to be dropped off and picked up for Brisbane. When we had returned to Townsville, after our leave, the colonel contacted us and ordered us to report to Officer School! We were the first soldiers recommended for Officer School in our battery."

"Comer, what an honor! They recognized that you were a great leader then?" I asked. Comer beamed at me. The memory still brought him delight and pride.

"Yes, finally! So we went for the physical exam. Both of us were found to have chronic malaria, high blood pressure, and a heart murmur! So we were disqualified. They sent us to the hospital for six months to treat the malaria. They wanted to reexamine us in six months, and we hoped then we would be satisfactory for officer school. Now, those six months were a pleasure. We lounged in the hospital with no duties to speak of, a quite nice private room. We could come and go as we pleased, as long as we were back in the hospital at night. We went to bars, nightclubs, the race track. We had a good time!

"Well after six months they sent us back for another evaluation which was plumb foolishness. Malaria stays with you for seven years! So we were disqualified again, and told to stay in the hospital another six months. Of course, we never passed the physical, and so after that they assigned us to a leave area where boys would go till they could get on a ship to return to New Guinea.

"First they brought both of us in front of the reassignment board. They couldn't send us back to Milne, too concerned about the malaria. So Bill was to go in to be reassigned and then me. I told him when he went in, 'Now you be sure to tell them that we want to be assigned together. Tell them we are twins.' Do you know that fool brother of mine went in, got his assignment and never mentioned me? Well then it was my turn. I went in and I told the Colonel, 'That boy that was just in here- that was my twin brother. We have been through this war together all the way till now. The only way I will leave his side is if you put us in separate stockades.'"

At this point in his story, Comer could not speak. He looked to the right, as though he were seeing the brother, the twin piece of his own spirit, still standing there. He shook his head and swallowed, tears gathering in the corner of his eyes.

"The Colonel issued a standing order that we were never to be separated for the duration of the war." Comer paused and looked at me, his eyes glistening, "And we never were.

"We were placed in an outfit called U.S. Army Distribution. Our job was bivouacking supplies. My brother was in charge of putting soldiers from leave on and off the ship and I was in charge of the supplies. We had plenty of money. You know both Bill and I were very good poker players and we had stockpiled a good bit of cash from that. Also, we made money selling extra supplies. Each soldier was given a pack of cigarettes a week, but of course, not all of them smoked. So I would keep the cigarettes that were extra, and sell them to the boys who wanted more than their one pack. Back then a carton was about $1, but I got $10 a carton! I made some good money."

I knew from my egg calculations that he was getting the equivalent of $132.27 a carton in today's money. This was a shrewd businessman long before he ever became a millionaire.

"We knew a lady friend in charge of a champagne distributing plant," Comer continued.

"How did you know her?"

"Oh you know me and the ladies," winked Comer, "She wasn't a girlfriend, just a friend. Not like that pretty little girl I told you about before in Ipswitch. But I did have a very serious relationship at this time. I was head over heels for her."

I really was flabbergasted by Comer and all the women he had found during his war years. Having seen the pictures of him as a young man, and knowing what a charmer he still was, I understood why women threw themselves at him. Nonetheless, I only knew Comer in the context of his dutiful and passionate devotion to Evelyn. The night and day difference was a perplexing conundrum.

"Who was the woman you were head over heels in love with, Comer?"

"I'll tell you about her in a little while. First, the champagne lady. She would give us several bottles, and it was just impossible to get champagne during the war. She didn't give me many, or she would've gotten in trouble. But I would sell those bottles for $100 a piece!"

Between the eggs, cigarettes, and champagne, Comer was already worth more than my lifetime income.

"Was the army upset with you making money off supplies?"

"If they were, they never stopped me."

I waited to see if he had any moral concerns over making money off of his fellow soldiers, but he didn't seem to be bothered by this at all.

"We made money another way too," said Comer, "Australia is horse racing crazy. I got into horse racing gambling."

"You bet on horses?" I asked.

"No, I was the bookie. The race track let me take bets, and I got to keep any earnings. I paid them off when they won, but I kept the profits when they didn't. I made a lot of money. Anyway, I became friends with some of the horse owners. They belonged to the Australian mafia...it was like the mafia here. They had a horse, named Red Boy. Best horse over there. They let me have a small share in him. He was a great horse, won everything in sight. Anyway, one day, I placed a $10,000 bet on him."

I gasped. Based on my egg calculations, $10,000 in 1943 had to translate to $132,272 in today's value. That buys a lot of eggs, even today. Probably enough to clog the arteries of every man, woman, and child in America.

"Well, the horse was winning, he *always* won. But just before he crossed the line, the jockey pulled him up. He threw the race on purpose and Red Boy lost. I lost $10,000...but so did the Mafia owners and they were hopping mad. They shot and killed that jockey right in front of us before he even got off the race track."

And these folks were Comer's buddies.... Just for the record, I am sure the Australian mafia are very nice people. After all, who *wouldn't* murder the jockey for throwing the race and losing that fortune?

"My brother Bill and I played poker constantly, though, and that's how we got rich. If we were not downtown carousing, bar hopping, or girl chasing, we were playing poker. We earned $50,000 playing poker. I sent a lot home to my mom. The army would pay the mother of soldiers $100 a month. She bought some new furniture with that money. So with our $200 a month going to her, she was making out all right. But the army had made a mistake. They were only supposed to send $100 no matter how many soldiers were in a family. So they caught up with us and asked us to repay it. We told them to make us. They let it go. In war time, you can get away with anything." (especially when you are best buds with the Australian mafia, which again, I am sure are *very nice people*.)

"Did they *want* you playing poker?" (You cannot pay enough money to find the kind of investigative acumen that this author must possess to be able to come up with these kinds of perceptive questions.)

"Not for the kind of money we were playing for. They told us to stop but we didn't. Anyway, there were a lot of good rec halls and dance halls for soldiers. It was a very enjoyable time. I got serious about a couple of girls. You know about the girl in Brisbane. After I went to Sidney for our exams for Officer School, we often went to the hotel bars. They had beautiful lounges in the hotels. I would go in the afternoons, and on the weekends. Well one day I was passing by one, and I said, 'I believe I will go in.' I wasn't wearing a uniform, which was punishable by jail. But I didn't like them. I didn't look good in them. So I had my own tailor made, much more flattering. Wore that one till they caught me."

I laughed, picturing that dapper, proud young man making his own uniform that gave him a jauntier appearance. The poor Army! They had no idea what they were trying to tame when they got a hold of Comer Hawkins!

"You looked mighty fine in that tailored suit, didn't you?"

"I do believe I did," he agreed.

"Did they send you to jail?"

"No, you can do...."

"I know...anything in wartime," I finished for him.

"That's right!" he said grinning, "Well so I went in and I saw two beautiful ladies. I introduced myself. One was quite friendly and one was aloof. 'May I sit down?' I asked. We got along pretty well. I called my brother and told him I had met two beautiful girls and we were going to take them out that night. Now the aloof one was the Australian Brigadier General's wife. His name was Gen. X."

(For the record, his name was not really General X. But given what you are about to hear, I am in dangerous waters, trolling for a major lawsuit from any surviving members of General X's family. Since I don't have their permission to expose their great grandmother for her wartime indiscretions, I will tell you that Comer's story is true, but General X and his wife will remain un-named, except in code.)

"He was serving in Egypt at the time. His wife was the most beautiful woman I had ever seen. She had been born in Russia, and escaped. After leaving Russia, she had settled in Australia. Anyway, she belonged to the Russian Club and it was the most wonderful club in Sydney. It was something else, let me tell you! I was only one of two Americans allowed to actually join the club, because I would come in with the General's wife."

I gawked at Comer. This was the faithful partner of 65 years to Evelyn! I saw nothing in his post-war years or his current life that would have clued me in to the illicit passions of his single days during the war.

"You dated a married woman?" I croaked.

"Everyone did!" he said, "That was expected. I lived with her for several months. The General found out about it. You know what he told me?"

"I can't imagine," I said, knowing the "G" rating of my book was in serious jeopardy. I had so wanted this to be a nice Disney story of war, one the whole family could curl around, but it was rapidly degenerating into the kind of books one reads under the sheet with a flashlight.

"He told me I better take good care of her. I told him I would. I was madly in love."

"Did he come and tell you that himself?" I asked, incredulous.

"No, he sent a lieutenant to my apartment. He said he knew I was friends with Mrs. X- that was the General's wife. He told me, 'The General said if you don't treat his wife nice, he'll come kick your ass.' It was accepted, even approved. The Generals were gone from home for years! I told him, 'I love this woman. You don't need to worry."

He must have noticed the shock on my face because he added, "I know, it was shameful...but that was expected in war. She would have left her husband, but I knew that in the end, I wasn't going to bring her back to the United States...and I didn't want to stay in Australia.

"But she was so beautiful, I could hardly believe she was human. She had alabaster skin, short shiny hair in a bob...she looked like Hedy Lamar. Do you know Hedy Lamar?" he asked, pausing and looking up.

"I know she was beautiful," I said.

"I was quite the ladies' man," admitted Comer, "I was always a gentleman though, except for when I was knocking heads..... There was a doctor I was friends with and he had a beautiful daughter. I dated her some, but nothing serious. Bill and I had a room in an apartment, and down the hall was a professional dance girl. I liked her, but I never did get with her. I don't know why. I think it could have been because of her father...."

He paused to consider this enigma for a while. The clock ticked and the recorder read-out showed me we'd been talking for three hours. Given what he was telling me about his wartime love affairs, was he serious about wondering why any father would want to keep him as far from his daughter as possible?

"I think it was because her father wouldn't let her have anything to do with Americans," Comer concluded.

Yes, that must be it....

"He threatened me that if he ever caught me with his daughter, he'd kill me. So I stayed away from her. But I did tell him that if he ever tried to assault me, I'd kill him."

Comer glanced at me, and added, "Of course, I wouldn't have killed him, but he didn't know that."

(Frankly, I didn't know that either, but I kept that to myself.)

"Now at that Russian Club, they had some amazing entertainment. One night, an aborigine came to sing a popular song from the time. It was called *Mauri Farewell*. Do you know that song? Well anyway, they put that little aborigine in a suit, and sent him out on stage with his big frizzy hair. Quite comical. But then he started to sing in a big baritone voice, a beautiful voice. He knew only one word of English, outside of the songs. 'Unbelievable'. That was the only English he could speak, but oh, he could sing.

"Well, we left that first apartment and rented a big brownstone, the whole upper floor of it. It had two bedrooms, a bath and a parlor. It was at King's Cross, that is part of Sydney. My brother and I paid $12 a week for that place." *(or just a little more than one egg.)*

"We'd come in at night and the owner would have a big fire going for us. We enjoyed it very much. Around that time, they offered me a field promotion to 2nd Lieutenant. I would be assigned to a small island hopping boats supplying to the upper combat front. I would sail up the Coral Sea, deliver supplies. But half the boats never made it! Half were sunk by the subs. Small little boats. I hated the ocean and I didn't want to get on that boat. So I resigned the commission. That was not long before we were discharged.

"See, depending on how many battles you engage in and how much time was served, you would get points. When you had enough points you could go home, discharged on points. My brother and I had more points by far than anyone else there."

"You saw a lot of combat," I said.

"Yes," he said simply. No wonder the man sought solace in gambling, women, and carousing. How does one face death every day for four years and emerge unscathed?

"I was still several months away from when I did get discharged, so I went back to the leave area where I was assigned. Do you know with all those years as gun commander, and all that time serving as acting Sergeant, I never got promoted to Sergeant? Well my captain found out and promoted me to staff Sergeant. When I was discharged just a short time later, he asked me if I would give the rank back since I was going home."

"Were they only allowed a certain number of promotions?"

"Yes," answered Comer, "And I knew I was leaving. I didn't need it. So I gave it back. I was promoted, but not discharged with it."

What a selfless action that had been for Comer, who had longed throughout the whole war to be made Sergeant. No wonder the mafia and his men and the Australians and the ladies loved him. Who could not love him, this good and kind and generous man? Maybe the seeds of the man he would become were already there, even if he did have a tendency to split skulls now and then.

"Now there was one little incident...let's see...how should I put this?" He paused and considered how he should tell me the story that seemed to be a delicate one.

What could be causing such reticence given that he had freely told me about charging soldiers for cigarettes, selling bootleg champagne for $100 a bottle, living with the General's wife, and joining the mafia in owning a race horse?

"One little instance I need to tell you about. As previously stated, my brother was in charge of putting the vacationing soldiers on ships back to their stations. Well, some of the boys weren't showing up. It was getting to be a problem."

"You mean they were going AWOL?"

"Right. One little Italian was in the mob from Cleveland. He was a tough guy. Nice fellow, but tough guy. Well he told me, 'If you keep me down here, I'll find those boys and bring them back.' So we did. We had him help us find the boys that were trying to hide. He found several and brought them back. One boy he couldn't find. He was gone several weeks, maybe longer.

"Anyhow, a fellow with a girlfriend in another town went to visit her and saw that fellow. He had gotten married, was working in a factory and his wife was having a baby! So the Italian from Cleveland came back to me and told me he'd found the fellow and told me where he was. 'Do you want me to get him?' he asked me. I told him, 'What's one soldier? You never found him.' "

Comer's voice broke and he swabbed some tears away. *That's* the man I knew, hiding in the soldier's hard shell.

"It was just one soldier," added Comer, his voice cracking, "Who would miss him?"

But the wife and the baby would've missed him, I thought, smiling at my tender, old friend. I was glad there were some heads he was unwilling to knock.

"Sometimes we would go to Ipswitch on leave, and it was just a small town with three little pubs. One was significantly better than the other two. It was an Americanized bar. Pubs served mostly beer. Australians were not really 'spirits' drinkers. The main pub, the Americanized one was frequented by the merchant marines, Aussies, and the Americans. One night, a very beautiful American girl showed up at the pub. Now we were all surprised. What was an American girl doing there? She told us that she was just visiting, but I was suspicious. She was very pleasant, very conversational.

Naturally, every man there tried to cozy up to her, but not me. I *knew* she wasn't supposed to be there. Each night, she would pick a target to victimize, usually a merchant marine. She always picked an officer if one was present. The supply ship marines were a unit by themselves. Each night she would leave with one, take him to her apartment, and seduce him. She would ply him with drinks, and ask pertinent questions.

"During this same time period, we were losing a lot of the merchant marine cargo ships in the Coral Sea. They were being sunk by the Japanese subs and we couldn't figure out why so many. Well after three of her victims ended up getting their ships sunk, we were putting it all together.

"So they dressed an investigative officer as a marine chief petty officer. He was a personable, handsome guy. His job was to cozy up to her. She fell for it. He hinted enough for her to know where a nonexistent ship would be sailing. So the boys calculated enough time for a submarine to get into position on the supposed ship's track, and they dive bombed it. They blasted that sub to heaven and back. Everyone knew now who was the informant. They arrested her and put her in the stockade till they could conclude she was guilty. She never gave her name. Never found her address or who she was. She was tried and convicted of destruction of naval property and loss of able bodied seamen. Condemned to death. I always suspected her of wrong doing. I knew she was not American."

How uncanny that this inveterate ladies' man was discerning enough that he did not pursue this one 'pretty little girl', this one who turned out to be a traitor. It seems she was the *only* pretty little girl he did not pursue.

"Another time, Bill was at our favorite pub and about midnight, the military police brought him home, all beat up. One eye was completely closed, his lip was swollen and split, he had internal bruising. There were five men living in our encampment there at the time. We all knew we had to do something. The next morning another fellow showed up and told us he knew who had done this to Bill. So he led us to the place where he knew the fellow would be.

"The two merchant marines who were responsible were sitting at the end of the bar. The witness told us, 'That's them.' So the five of us hemmed them. They tried to get up but we grabbed them by their collars and their hair, and marched them out the door. The bartender called the MPs, but in the meantime, those tall, mean, New England buddies of mine belted the marine, punched him good in the solar plexus, then slammed him good and hard in both eyes. His partner grabbed the other marine and whacked him.

"The MPs came, hand cuffed the marines. They knew we were in the right. They charged the merchant marines with assault and battery, and robbery too. They had stolen Bills's wallet, watch and knife. Just before they put them in the patrol car, the MP handed me his billy club. I took the club and slammed the one that had beaten my brother between his neck and collar bone.

"Most merchant marines were good and honorable," said Comer, "We couldn't have won the war without them. But these were bad eggs! "

While I was busy envisioning just how hard my gentle friend had bashed the Merchant Marine, Comer switched gears.

"Did I ever tell you about my favorite lounge in Brisbane? I had a pretty interesting experience there. I went to my favorite lounge for a drink. Naturally, I saw a pretty little girl. I bought her a drink, took her to dinner, and when we finished, she said she had a private beach about ten minutes away by tram. She told me it was a very beautiful beach, moonlit. Would I like to take a stroll? So I said, 'Sure!'

"To get to the beach from the street, we had to go down some stairs. She kept glancing back over her shoulder. Then I realized, this is a set-up! I saw a fellow sneaking down the stairs. I always carried a sharp sheathe knife in my sleeve. I had practiced pulling it out fast countless times. So I grabbed her hair and got out my knife. Every Alabaman man knew how to use a knife. The 'Alabama slash' is to take the thumb and forefinger, and slash little cuts without killing. So she yelled to the guy, 'Stay back! He's got a knife!' The attacker stopped- he was an Aussie civilian. With my pointed blade, I jabbed her in the rear, just a little. I marched her back up the stairs to the tram stop. I held her there until the tram came, then I got back on and left.

"I saw her in the same bar, several weeks later. She told me she was sorry, that the attacker made her do it. And you know what, I believed her. She also told me, 'I got two pretty little scars on my rear.' I told her I didn't want to see them. People tried to take advantage of the soldiers who were trying to save the country. I never could understand that."

Neither could I. I am sure if they had examined Comer's wartime antics a little more carefully, they would have found some other soldier to mess with.

"We were set on a famous racetrack where we encamped in Brisbane, just 15 miles into Sidney where we lived. The trains ran about 70 mph, but they had lots of drop off stations. I often took the trains back and forth from Sidney. One time, I was on the train, and instead of making a lot of stops, like it usually did, this time we noticed that we were flying by them. Some Aussie soldier said, 'Something's wrong!'. He went up front to see what it was. The driver was dead! Died of a heart attack! The Aussie knew what to do and he pulled the train to a stop just two stations from Sidney. It would have been a disaster, if it would have slammed into the Sidney stations!"

That would have been an ironic tragedy, for my friend to have survived the hundred or so bombing raids only to die aboard a runaway train. The countless times Comer had been preserved struck me as nothing short of miraculous. If Comer had not made it, who would be holding Evelyn's hand now as she struggled through the onslaught of Alzheimers? I couldn't imagine anyone being more loving, gentle, or faithful than the man who had been such an incorrigible soldier. Who would ever have imagined it? I was still trying to reconcile the image of the remorseless soldier who stabbed, jabbed, and smacked his way through the war with the kind neighbor who never raised his voice, and always had an irrepressible grin on his face. He was not the most likely of candidates for sainthood, not back then.

"So our time was almost up and we were making oodles of money. There was a lucrative black market, but I never got into that. The big bad boys were the ones in *that* market."

Comer saw fit to draw the line at something! Thus far there had been little indication that there was anything he wouldn't do, since in war, "you can do anything." I guess even this irrepressible gambler, hustler, and lady-chasing carouser knew there was a line he shouldn't cross.

"Oil and tires. Severe punishment if you were caught dealing in oil and tires.," said Comer, "One fellow asked me to get him some gas. I told him, no! Next time he saw me, he asked me for tires. Again, I told him no. Now I did have control of the cigarettes, but I wasn't stealing them. I would buy them back from the soldiers that didn't want them, or some gave me them as gifts. Anyway, back to this fellow. I hailed a cab and had one foot in, and this fellow opened the door from the other side with a gun in his hand! I jumped back and fell in the street. The cab pulled off with that fellow in it, and I made myself scarce.

"That fellow once slashed a friend of mine. I had another friend who was a tough guy, mean and strong. I asked him to go 'remind that gun toting fellow of the error of his ways'. So my friend went and beat him up, broke some bones. The bad guy never bothered us again.

"One other time, my 'enforcer' friend helped me out. We had the cigarette business going but as supply officers, we could control that. One guy had a pushcart and he sold meatballs...they were delicious....Anyway, he also started cutting into my cigarette business. I told him to stop but he wouldn't. My 'enforcer' went to the pushcart boy, and roughed him up. He turned over the pushcart and it caught on fire. That was the end of the fellow cutting into my cigarette business." he laughed, shaking his head and picturing the yummy meatballs rolling in the street with his adversary.

"It was brutal, wasn't it?" I asked, really at a loss for words. Comer told the stories so cavalierly. He did not appear to feel any guilt over the savagery of his exploits.

"War is horrible," said Comer, as though reading my mind, "There is never a good reason for war. By this time, we had our points we needed for discharge, and Bill and I, we were ready to go home. We had had enough. We had been there four years, and we had 104 points. Only one other guy in the whole theatre had more. Brother Bill and I, we were the first two soldiers sent home on points. They sent us to Miami for rehab, but they put us up in a plush hotel. So many pretty girls in Miami! I am sorry to say, I wasn't totally faithful to General X's wife."

CHAPTER SIX
BACK IN THE STATES

"Well!" I said happily to Comer, "That ends the war for you! What happened in Miami?"

"The army put both Bill and me in the Sands Hotel. It was quite a plush hotel. We were sent there at first for rehab, you know, some R and R for the returning soldiers. It was quite a nice place and we enjoyed it there very much. I was wondering why they were spending that kind of money on us to stay at such a nice hotel. Unbeknownst to me, a good boyhood pal was in military intelligence in Miami. He knew we were coming, and he is the one who had arranged for us to be placed in that fine hotel! He said, 'I'm gonna let you work with me.' The other boys coming home often came with wads of money, and they were getting mugged. My friend wanted me to help catch the muggers. So he gave me money to flash around, setting me up as a 'Judas goat'. He said, 'Someone is going to come after you.'

"So, I pretended to be drunk, and sure enough, right away, here comes a mugger! My friend comes out, orders his arrest, and the mugger ran. So my friend shot him! Not to kill him. He shot him in the buttocks. But that was all I wanted of that duty. I asked my friend to let me be relieved of assisting with the muggers."

I had thought that with Comer back in the USA, the gruesome violence would be over. I had hoped now we'd be on our way learning how to become a millionaire. But it was not to be. Comer had not yet worked all the kinks out of his character.

"So then, I was a desk clerk at the Sands Hotel. That way, they could say I was being useful. I was in Miami for eight weeks. The Sands Hotel offered me a permanent job, but I thanked them, and requested reassignment.

"Brother Bill and I had to go back for another physical exam then. Bill failed again and was discharged. I didn't fail so I was reassigned to a Mississippi POW camp as a military policeman. The town was way out in the country. I worked there till my final discharge eight months later.

"I was in charge of the POWs cutting up pulpwood. They were German POWs. The funny thing was, those Germans treated me as a friend. They held no animosity. They told me, 'We had no choice! It wasn't our war! Hitler was a brutal murderer.' Most of those POWs hated Hitler. The war wasn't ended yet. I was still in the service when the bomb dropped."

Comer seemed surprised that the enemy was likable. It was easy to think of the enemy as a whole country of maniacs who deserved to die. It was much harder to picture them as boys who hated their leader as much as he did, and were forced to fight. This story was perhaps more disturbing than all the others. Those poor boys, pawns in a game they didn't want to play and would not win.

Was this one of the incidents that began to challenge the warrior spirit in Comer that had so gallantly and ferociously blasted away at the enemy? It certainly seemed to have made an impact on him.

"But those German soldiers watched over me. When it was cold, they would build me a bonfire. I never worried about them hurting me. If they finished their quota of work, we got to go back to the barracks. They would work hard, finish early, and we could go back early and just enjoy ourselves. It was glorious. A nice little town, nice people, and the POWs were great guys.

"There *was* one fellow who was rebellious. He was the one fellow in the group who was a Nazi. He kept losing his tools and holding us up for an hour while we looked for them. Finally, I told them, 'He's your man. Do what you want with him.' They trounced him, and he stopped leaving his tools behind.

"We were done at 2:00 every day and the bus would come and take us to the barracks. One day, he didn't show up until 6:00! We stood in the rain four hours waiting for him. When he came, I punched him with my rifle butt. Knocked out his teeth. He wouldn't drive the bus any more. He reported me to the Colonel!"

Comer seemed genuinely surprised by this. In Comer's eyes, there was no doubt the bus driver deserved to lose his teeth over that.

"What did the Colonel do?" I asked, "Throw you in the brig?"

"Heck no!" said Comer, "He asked me what my complaint had been, and I told him. He agreed with me. Our new bus driver was always on time after that."

(And I bet he wore a mouth guard and helmet if he knew what was good for him.)

"We had a good place to go on weekends, a nice little club. Let me tell you about that. An American soldier came to me and told me, 'We need to build a nightclub and bar.' I asked him how. He said, 'Leave it to us.' Well those soldiers went out and loaded a truck with stolen lumber, supplies, and window frames...for a month. Then they worked every night for another month building the club. We had to buy the plumbing, couldn't find that just lying around, and built quite a nice little bathroom. One fellow was a cabinet maker who made us a half circle bar, real nice, cause he was an expert builder. Somebody even found us a jukebox! An old farmer had land that he let us build on. He knew he would get the building when we left. It was a beautiful club! About 30 x 20 foot room. Our little night club hosted many parties. A very attractive place, windows, nice bathroom.

"However, I still would go to town. There was a 'special attraction' in town."

He smiled, and I strongly suspected I was going to hear another 'pretty little girl' story.

"Back then, they had what they called 'road houses'. I went there with some friends. I saw a girl dancing on the dance floor. I was mesmerized. I couldn't believe I'd seen such a pretty girl! My date got upset."

(*no kidding?*)

"Anyhow, when we were driving home, we saw a wreck on the road, so we stopped. This girl, the one that mesmerized me, was lying in the road. Another fellow took her to the hospital. The next day I called the hospital..."

"Of course you did!" I laughed.

"But she wasn't there anymore. A week later, a fellow asked me to go home and play bridge with him. They needed a fourth player, and he knew I played bridge. He told me, 'I got a girl joining us.' Well, guess who that girl was?"

"The pretty little girl?" I said.

"You got it! So she was my new love. I stayed with her for eight months. Her daddy had an oil well. She wanted me to stay, but then, I was discharged from the army, and I wanted to go back to Georgia. She was married...claimed she was separated from her husband, but I didn't care. She was really nice.

"When we were discharged, the army gave me $100. That was all the money I had. I went into town, and in one night spent all that money! I think I told you before I squandered it all on wine, women, and song. Didn't even have the cash to get a taxi to take me home. For the time being, I was now out of the army, 25 years old, and flat broke."

I knew that Comer did not remain flat broke. I asked him how he went from destitute to millionaire. I took careful notes in case his plan could be replicated.

"I made my way to Atlanta, where my brother Bill was a claims manager for Mutual of Omaha Insurance company. I didn't want to go into insurance, so at first, I worked for the highway department, as an engineering aid. It was enjoyable work, but low salary.

"Since my brother worked in the insurance field, I gave that a try. I got licensed by Mutual of Omaha, and started making money. I made a good start, good promotions to duties and titles. I became an agent, then a special agent, and then a sales manager. Finally they gave me my own agency. A third of Georgia was my territory. In two to three years, I had 35 agents working for me. It was getting to be lucrative.

"After 18 months, the home office decided to merge my agency with another, and offered me a sales manager job. That would have been a come down, so I turned it down. At that same time, Progressive Life insurance asked me to be an Agency Director, so I took that. I set up general agencies all across the state. I worked there for a year.

"At that time, Piedmont Central bought Progressive Life, and again offered me a sales job. I turned that one down. Then Brinks offered me a job as their Southern Rep. They wanted me to make contracts, sell business with federal banks. I kept that job for five years.

"While working at Brinks, I decided to go to law school. I went to school in the evenings and weekends for three and a half years. I didn't have a college education, but in those days, you could go into law school without one. Anyway, I went to Woodrow Wilson College of Law in Atlanta. I was the top student in my class, top five anyway, out of 150 students. The dean came to me after just two years and certified me to take the Bar exam. I was the only one to take it before finishing my degree. I took it with a group of 400 people. Out of 400 people, only 17% passed. But not me.

"Now I *knew* I had passed. I knew the answers, and I knew I had done well. For so few to have passed, we all felt something fishy was going on, and it caused a huge outcry. Finally we found out that the Bar Association had decided there were too many lawyers, so they decided how many could pass. Some people were announcing they passed before the results were posted, so we knew there had been some sort of collusion.

"That left a mighty bad taste in my mouth, but I went on and finished and got my degree. I didn't take the Bar again. Of all people, the dean encouraged me not to practice law. He told me I had real promise and I was never going to make real money as a lawyer. He told me to go into another field. It was one of those blessings in disguise. I ended up in a whole different field for most of my life, and it was work I loved. And I became a millionaire doing it. Not passing the Bar was probably the best thing that could've happened to me!"

Turning Points * Vicky Kaseorg

Comer Hawkins- 1959

This is a common phenomenon in the stories of successful people. What looks at first like devastating setback, abject failure, irredeemable catastrophe, turns out to be the pivot upon which victory swings. Surprisingly, despite Comer's conviction that he had been treated shabbily by the Bar, he seemed to be over his head-knocking approach to adversity. He didn't bash a single bar reviewer with the butt of his rifle over the unfair treatment. Like any good poker player, Comer knew when to fold. Comer was changing.

"Pittston bought Brinks, but they didn't 'buy me', so I was out of a job again. Well at that time, with all my sales experience, Merrill Lynch was looking at me. They offered me a job, but I had met first with the managing partner of another brokerage firm called 'Courts and Company'. Courts and Company hired me on the spot. They told me they couldn't afford *not* to hire me!

"Now to become a stock broker, first you have to work six months and then you take an exam. After four months, Courts told me, 'Take the exam early.' I hadn't even studied, but they locked me in a room to take the test. Took all day to finish it! And I passed! I was the only person to take it after only four months of working. They knew about all my experience hiring people. So I opened the first suburban office in Atlanta. Me and another fellow opened a little office in Lenox Square. It is one of the biggest shopping centers in the country.

"We started that office, and hired more and more men. Then we moved to a bigger place in Phipps Plaza. Built that in a year up to 16 men, then in two years to

35 men. I stayed there another four years, but then I needed more space. So I opened a bigger office, hired more men. I was with them 25 years, and then the suburban and downtown offices merged. They brought someone in from Fort Lauderdale to manage it, and after 25 years, I decided it was time to retire."

"Comer!" I cried, "You skipped over the most riveting part of your tale! When and how did you meet Evelyn?"

"I was saving the best for last," he said, with a grin, "I had already started working with Courts and Company. I had a friend from Puerto Rico, very wealthy guy. He was very influential and he had three sons and a daughter. He sent the kids to America to go to school. The Puerto Rican girl became friends with Evelyn. The Puerto Rican girls in the family all went to Pharmacy School there. Anyway, my friend asked me one day, 'Let's go watch some girls bowl! I know this one girl who is very good. You will like watching.'

So we went to the bowling alley, and there was Evelyn. She was the best bowler I had ever seen in real life. She was really good. And she was so confident. And very pretty. I knew from the moment I saw her that she was special."

Turning Points * Vicky Kaseorg

She had to be pretty special, to have bowled Comer over, with his past of courting the most beautiful girls in the South Pacific. I gazed at her picture- the gorgeous, dark haired Evelyn with her hourglass figure,

Evelyn bowling - 1948

and perfect bowling form, her neat waist cinched with a belt and a full a-line skirt billowing around her shapely legs. I totally understood why Comer was smitten. What I didn't understand was how she could bowl in a dress.

Turning Points * Vicky Kaseorg

"The next day, the Puerto Rican family asked me and my brother Bill to go to a family picnic. We both had dates...in fact, they were sisters. I had a good time there, and guess who was there? Evelyn! She didn't have a date. I was infatuated. You know, I don't remember if I asked her out right then and there...but I must have. Somehow, we got together, and from that day on, Evelyn was my girl.

"Evelyn was only 23. I was 31 when I met her. She was a U.S. Air-force recruiting model. Her picture was splashed all over the country! Then she became secretary to the head of the General Service Administration and kept that job all the way till Angie, our daughter, was five years old.

"Anyway, she was a very likable person, very pretty. Never fussed, never disagreed. I suppose we had our tiffs, but I don't remember any."

I was already jealous of Evelyn. A model, an accomplished bowler who could bowl in a dress, and to top it all off, she was nice. I wanted the legacy Evelyn had, at least the character if not the lovely legs. I wondered what she had seen in this wild man who had so recently been sabering the shoulders of superior officers. Not only was Evelyn gorgeous, and nice...she apparently had prescience of the man Comer would become.

"Did you know you wanted to marry her right away?" I asked.

"From the moment I met her," said Comer.

"Did she know about all your 'pretty little girls'?"

"No, she never asked and I never told her. But you know, once I met Evelyn, she was the only girl for me. No more 'pretty little girls'. When I got married, I was *married*, if you know what I mean."

I did, and I was glad. Something again was changing Comer, and it appeared to be love. I was glad that after all the destruction, devastation, and tumult of the war, and malaria, and poverty, my friend found solace in the love of his life.

"But I figured I didn't have enough money to get married," Comer said, "I was determined to give up gambling, but I wanted to do one more thing with it first. I told Evelyn, when I raised another $5,000, we would get married. Now remember, I was a great poker player. In fact, I had a very good friend, he was connected with the Mafia, but he was a great poker player. Won Vegas! Well, he wrote a book on gambling, and said there were only two people in the world he couldn't beat, and that was the Hawkins boys." (*I am sure the Las Vegas mafia are very nice people too...*)

"You are in his book?" I asked.

"Yep, he never beat either of us. I was a better player than Bill. Bill was too reckless. I won using common sense. Anyway, I admit I kind of double crossed Evelyn."

"What do you mean?"

"Well, I won that $5000 right away, but I still waited two or three months before we got married. I didn't know if $5000 would be enough to give her the best life I could give her, so I kept gambling till I thought I had enough. And then we got married, and I never gambled again."

The knocking head days were over, the carousing was over, and now the gambling was over. Enemies turned into friends, a woman worth forsaking all else entered his world, and the desire to live an honest life with her ended his gambling career. Milne Bay was only one of many turning points.

"We spent our whole life in Atlanta, till I retired in 1988, and moved here in 2000. My daughter Angie was born in 1955. She was a good baby. We went to 'baby school' to learn how to care for her, how to raise her. They had schools like that back then. I bathed her, which was my job." He smiled wistfully, looking off into the distance, and I imagined he was picturing those bucolic days and hearing the sounds of a baby cooing and gurgling as she splashed her hands in the tub.

"Comer, if you could do your life all over again, what would you change?" I was very curious to see if he would renounce his bashing superiors, his pretty little girls, his cozying up with the Mafia...even his exorbitant spending spree on eggs.

Comer was silent for a moment, "You know, I don't know how to answer that. I just took things as they came and dealt with them. I have never been unhappy. I learned at an early age that you have to accept what fate gives you and make the best of it."

I knew this was true. Despite his wife being in an Alzheimer's unit, slowly losing her memory of the life they had shared, despite his multiple strokes, and double vision for twenty years, and his once vigorous body needing to stumble slowly along using a cane, he was always grinning. He held his ailing wife's hand, patting it tenderly, as I would drive them through the Charlotte neighborhoods, finding it an inestimable joy to still be beside her gazing together at a world that was slowly closing in around them. If anyone had managed to make the best of it, my friend Comer had.

"I always liked to help people...though I was a trouble maker at times as a young man. But I did more charity work as an adult than anyone else I know. I took care of old folks, and headed up the charity division of a business club I was in. I organized donations to disadvantaged men. I remember one time we did a drive to get them ties. Some mighty nice ties were donated! I even kept one I really liked. I used to fill my station wagon with food and bring it to poor families. I remember being really touched that some of those kids didn't even have shoes.

"If I could be remembered for just one thing, it would be that I did more good than I did harm. And the thing I was most proud of was finding my wife and getting married. Nothing surpasses that. The second thing was the birth of my daughter. With them, I had everything I wanted. Anything else was anti-climatic after that!

"But what would I do differently? Hmmm. I have some regrets, but no remorses."

"What do you mean?" I asked, "What is the difference?"

"Well regrets are little things, you know your intolerances, or shortcomings. Remorse is deeper, feeling shamed over what you have been. In the end, one finds happiness by a life fulfilled with family, success, and no remorses."

"What is the best we can do with our life, Comer?" I really wanted to know what he thought. He had lived a long life, and one that was filled with inconsistencies. But he had something very special that many of us do not have. He seemed to have found joy no matter what the circumstances. He found it while bombs were falling like confetti around him, while befriending the enemies he had once hoped to kill, and while dancing in the warm Australian breeze with a new partner each night. And now, impossibly, he found joy sitting with his ailing wife of sixty some years, having been faithful, hard working, honest, and charitable, and rewarded with watching Alzheimers slowly invade her mind. I wanted to know very much what this man thought was the secret to a good life.

"Be tolerant, be considerate with others and do unto others as you would have them do unto you."

Turning Points * Vicky Kaseorg

One could do much worse than to live by the Golden Rule.

"Any failures in life?" I asked.

"Well the two that I most think of are when I wanted to be a pilot, but I failed the eye test for air cadet school. And the second was when I failed to get in to officer candidate school because of malaria."

"But those aren't really personal failures...those are because your body failed you."

"True, and in the end, I thought I wanted to be a pilot, but I discovered, I really didn't. I did want to be an officer, and by the end of the war, however briefly, I was."

"Were you ever frightened in life?"

"I suppose the only time I was ever in danger in my life was during the war. With 101 bombing raids, sometimes 100 bombs falling at the same time...that was pretty frightening, but you know, I got used to it. After a while, I didn't really think of it as frightening. I just had a job to do and I focused on that job. I paid attention, and it all came out all right. Oh my, it is almost 5:00. I better get going now. It is time for me to head downstairs and feed Evelyn."

CHAPTER SEVEN
MALARIA

There was yet another turning point in Comer's life, and that had to do with malaria. One sixth of the forces on Milne Bay were sickened by malaria. It was on its way to defeating the Allies before the Japanese even showed up. The commanders had not known how truly devastating the disease could be. The antimalarial medication was in short supply, and often not taken by the troops. They had known that it was endemic in the area, but the precautions to prevent malaria in the troops were bordering on negligence. Rather than covering their skin, the troops rolled up sleeves or went shirtless in the wilting heat. Many man arrived without mosquito nets. The mosquito repellent was ineffective against that ravenous New Milne brand of blood suckers. Quinine, which was effective, was in short supply, and often taken too late after the men already had the disease, if taken at all. Many troops were told to wait a week before taking the medicine, for some inexplicable reason. By then, of course, the rapacious mosquitoes had infected many of them.

When I told Comer that I had read that one sixth of the men had malaria, he said, "Is that all? Seemed like more."

And it might have been more, had a tropical disease expert not showed up and insisted on new medicines and more aggressive prevention. Malaria was on the way to wiping out the entire force in Milne Bay.

We in the USA don't think much about malaria, but it is the 5th leading cause of death of all the infectious diseases worldwide, and second in Africa, after AIDS. (Center for Disease Control and Prevention). There are two kinds of malaria, essentially a less serious and a deadly type. Comer had the deadly type. His temperature had gone up to 106 degrees, when he was hospitalized in Australia. Few patients survive such a horrific onslaught.

"Malaria stays in your system seven years," Comer had told me, "It nearly killed me. On my wedding night, I went into a coma."

That is probably not the response the new bride was going for.

"What?!" I cried, "A coma? On your honeymoon? From malaria?"

"We were married in the afternoon. A very nice ceremony. A simple affair, a personal sort of thing. We were friends with the minister and it was really just a few of us and the minister. Then we had a reception at the Biltmore hotel. Well, I got to feeling bad, and then more and more feverish. It got worse and worse. Pretty soon, I had to call a cab to get me out of the hotel and he took me to my mother in law's house. That cabdriver had to carry me inside.

"I was in a semi-coma for three days. Terrible high fever, and chills. I don't remember anything of those three days. Evelyn and her mother bathed me with alcohol constantly to try and bring down the fever. You know, malaria is a very painful disease. Worse than anything. The pain is so bad, you want to scream. I had many attacks over the seven years, but this was the worst one except for when I almost died.

"But you know, that marriage attack was the last one I ever had. After those three days, I got up, and we went to New Orleans for our honeymoon."

I laughed, "End of malaria, start of marriage!"

"That's right," he said.

I had recently read the review of a book that described the emotional toll World War II took on the returning soldiers and their families. Despite many books that paint that generation of brave men and women as exceptional, and they were, most accounts do not deal with the tremendous residual effect of that brutal, prolonged conflict. Poor Comer had to endure seven years of illness, severe illness, as a reminder of the horrors of war. How grateful he must be with that turning point, and malaria finally vanquished as he started a new life with his wonderful bride.

"And how are you feeling now...with the stitches from the incision on your face?" I asked.

"Awful," he said, "On a scale of 1-10, about an 8 in pain."

"Comer, get some pain meds then!"

"I am having trouble getting them to come do what they are supposed to," he said, with uncharacteristic bitterness, "I'm supposed to have the bandage changed twice a day...I'm lucky if they show up once!"

"Well that isn't right," I said, "Have Angie raise a ruckus."

"She will," he said, "She just got back from out of town. I tell you, the past three days, a scale of ten wouldn't have been enough. I needed a scale up to 20 and the pain was an 18. I just huddled under a blanket on my recliner, and felt like I couldn't make it another hour. And then I just did, and managed the next hour. It was the worst three days of my life. Worse than malaria."

"Comer, you need to let your doctor know and get some pain meds that will help."

"I will tomorrow, Sugar, when I get the stitches out. But I gotta tell you another thing before you go. I go down each morning around 8:00 to meet Evelyn for breakfast. Usually they have all the residents in the parlor area, dressed and waiting for breakfast. I looked, and no Evelyn. So I went to her room, and she was on the floor, flat on her back, couldn't get up! She was wedged between the dresser and the bed. No telling how long she'd been there."

"She needs to come out with the others as soon as they dress her," I said, "So they can watch her."

"I told them that," said Comer, "I got mighty perturbed. But they are supposed to do that. I can tell them but that doesn't mean they'll listen."

Turning Points * Vicky Kaseorg

I knew that all in all, Comer loved the facility he was in. He found the staff kind and attentive. He told me many times that he had no complaints and was generally pleased with his new home. He must have been in a good deal of pain to be so uncharacteristically negative. And he must have been worried. No matter how attentive the aides were, it was almost impossible to prevent all falls when elderly people became weak and unsteady. Add a disintegrating mind to the mix, and it was a wonder poor Evelyn hadn't fallen more often!

"The man who knocked some heads with the butt of his rifle should be able to get them to listen," I offered.

"I did knock some heads in the war," he agreed, "Got a pretty funny story about butting heads," said Comer.

"No doubt," I said. I was glad to redirect his thoughts to those memories of when his strength was seemingly sufficient to deal with every problem that arose.

Communication was a problem at Milne Bay. While there was the radio tower for incoming planes transmission and radar, ground communication was limited to cable telephones, or at times, even human runners. The mucky, muddy ground and torrential rain made building and maintaining reliable signals equipment impossible. Comer prefaced his story telling me there were no radios or walkie-talkies for the men in the gun pits.

"So how did you communicate with your commanding officers?" I asked.

"Well I had a field telephone. We had sturdy cables that connected our telephones to the command office, and also to the other gun crews. It was MY telephone. No one was allowed to touch my telephone without my permission. After a bombing raid, the first call I always made was to gun pit #3, where my brother Bill was. After I knew he was safe, I would let my crew use the telephone all day if they wanted.

"Anyway, one time a new replacement had come in, and he didn't know my telephone rule. We had a bombing raid and when it ended, he jumped on my telephone. 'Watch this,' whispered one of my crew men, cause he knew what my reaction would be.

"I bounced my gun butt off that new recruit's head and he learned his lesson. I told him, 'No one touches my phone till I give permission.' "

"That's the Comer that needs to go make sure they take good care of Evelyn," I said, laughing.

CHAPTER EIGHT

A REVELATION

"I don't really have any more stories to tell you," Comer said, "But I would like to tell you about a short story I wrote. I would like very much for you to take the outline of the story, and write it for me. Embellish it. And then publish it."

I settled into my interview chair, in Comer's little parlor. I knew we were winding down on the stories that he remembered as being of particular interest. However, he would still tell me every time I called that there was some important story he needed to tell me, but it just wouldn't come to him.

I kept hoping he would remember it, but up to this point, he had not. Maybe today he will remember, I thought, as I entered his room.

"Did the war story you keep forgetting come to you yet?" I asked as I pulled out my notes.

"No. I suppose one day it will, but not yet."

I had heard so many gruesome tales by now, brutal escapades, horrific things...yet what I had not heard was expressions of fear. I know I would not have lasted a minute in Milne Bay. How had Comer? How does anyone deal with the fear?

"I do have a question for you before we get started," I said, "Were you afraid?"

"You have to remember," Comer told me, "After the big battle, we still suffered day after day of intense bombing raids. 101 bombing raids over the two years I was there. Every single bomb that fell was a potential death bomb. But we got used to it."

He had said that before, and I had accepted it. But now I realized that I didn't understand exactly what he meant by that. You get used to your kids losing enunciation skills when they become teenagers. You get used to the dogs barking at every passerby till your ears ring. You get used to looking in the mirror and wondering who that stranger is with sagging parts and wrinkles and what did she do with your face. You even get used to hot flashes that last ten years. You don't like them, but you get used to them. But how does one get used to 1,000 pound bombs falling all around you leaving pockmarks as big as a truck?

"Are you telling me you were not afraid?"

"No, the fear was *always* there. But you learn to live with it. For example, we all loved poker, and we would play poker the live long day. But if we had a red warning in the middle of a poker game, we would jump up and leave our money and our chips right where they were and hop into the gun pit. When the bombing raid was over, we would go back to our poker game. We were afraid, but we did our duty.

"The main thing we had to fear was what they called a tricky bomb. It was an anti-personnel bomb."

I laughed, "What a funny expression! Weren't all bombs '*anti-personnel*' bombs?"

"When that bomb came down, it sunk in the ground head first. And it had a three foot antennae sticking out. When the antennae hit the dirt, it triggered the explosion and it would spew shrapnel all around, killing anyone it could hit.

"So we stayed down in the slit trenches until the raid was over. Unless it was a direct hit, we were safe if we stayed below ground. But I will tell you, I was mighty scared when we were told to fix bayonets. We were all lined up in formation, with those shells whizzing overhead, and the Japanese not a half mile away. We knew we would be going into hand to hand fighting, and it was kill or be killed. I was very frightened then."

"How long did that last?" I asked.

"The whole day," he said, "The scariest day of my life."

I knew he was itching to tell me his short story. He had mentioned it a few times. He had told me all he had was the plot in his head and he wanted me to write it. He had conceived of the story after the war, but had never written it. However, I noticed he had no notes. He was ready to tell me this precious story, that he said was a really good one. I, on the other hand, did not want to take on another project. I knew my current batch of books would take months if not years to complete. I didn't need another story. I decided honesty was the best policy.

"Ok Comer, I will write down your outline, but I warn you, I can't work on more than one thing at a time, so it may be a long time before I get to writing it for you."

I felt bad. I knew Comer may very well not have a long time left, but I also knew that there was only so much I could do. One day I would write this story for him. But not yet. Writing his World War II story was stretching me to the limit already.

"Ok," said Comer, "That's fine. But it is a good story. I think you will like it."

"Then tell me. I'm ready," I said, turning to blank sheets of paper in my notebook crammed with his war tales.

"Well first there are two American pilots. They share a sleazy, dirty hospital room in enemy territory."

"Where?" I asked, "Where do you envision this hospital?"

"Viet Nam," he answered, "Now, one pilot had a window bed. He could look outside whenever he wanted. The other was in a corner bed, just looking on the walls. He had no view, and could not see out the window from where he was. They were friends. Each day his beloved comrade, the one with the window view, would describe hour by hour the sights out the window. It made the corner view soldier very happy. The window pilot would describe the seasonal changes. The leaves budding in the spring, turning green, the beautiful flowers opening in the sunshine. The birds building their nests. As summer comes, he would describe the thick foliage of the trees, the baby birds learning to fly, the flowers of summer, the azaleas and the roses."

Azaleas and roses in Viet Nam? I glanced up.

"You will know just how to describe it," said Comer, "You embellish as you see fit. Well, the window pilot described season after season, day after day. Every day he would tell the corner pilot what beautiful things were happening out the window. This went on for two years. And as time went by, the corner soldier became obsessed. All he lived for was to hear the description of what his beloved comrade was seeing out the window. And then, all he longed for was to one day have that window view. But he felt guilty about that desire because he knew the only way it would come to pass would be if his buddy died.

"As much as the corner pilot knew he wanted the window view, he also knew the only way to reach it would be the death of the other pilot. Well one day, the inevitable happens. The pilot with the window view dies. The flyer in the corner is heartbroken, but his consolation is that finally, after two long years, he will have the window bed. So the nurses come to move him to the window bed. The pilot closes his eyes, because when he opens them, he wants to have his first sight be that view he has obsessed over for so long."

"I know what happens," I broke in, chills raising the hair on my arms, "He opens his eyes and it is a brick wall. A dirty brick wall."

"How did you know that?" asked Comer, "It *is* a dirty brick wall with no view at all. He was so shocked and so dismayed that he feels his mind explode. He starts a horrible silent scream. By nightfall, he has lost his reason, but it doesn't matter anymore."

Here Comer stopped and looked at me. His face was bruised and swollen from the fifteen stitches he had had removed the day before. He smiled, a little wanly, his hands resting on his knees.

"What do you think?" he asked.

"I think you just told me what the war meant to you," I answered.

"But it wasn't about me," said Comer.

"All writer's stories are about the writer," I said, "Comer, what was the key to the corner pilot's desire to live?"

"I wanted to see beauty where there was none," said Comer.

"So you lived to hear the stories that gave you the hope of beauty," I said. I am not certain he had even noticed he had switched to personal pronouns.

"Yes, though of course it is a foregone conclusion there is no beauty in war."

"What about your pretty little girls?" I asked.

He perked up, "Yes, they were beautiful. But they weren't the war. War is not beautiful. There is no hope in war. It is not beautiful. It is ugly. I did what I had to do to survive, I did my duty."

"What was the window view you hoped for?" I asked.

Comer paused and looked at his gnarled hands.

"The reason to live, the hope of every soldier was that one day you'd get back home. You would see the flowers of home..."

Ah! The azaleas, the roses....

"And you would one day be married, have children. Just go home, and have all the things that home signified happen. That's what all soldiers dreamed of. Not just a view out a window, but the whole world. A view of home. If you couldn't have that, you'd be like the corner soldier, the one who never got to see the view."

"And who was the friend that showed you the view?" I asked softly.

"The view was imaginary," said Comer, thinking I had misunderstood his short story, "There was no view. We just wanted to survive that day...because we knew that the next day it would start all over again. When there was a lull, there was no relief. It was only temporary. You knew the next day you would have to face the bombs again. It was not going to end until the war ended."

"Comer, you were the gun crew commander. It must have been very hard to be the one who had to bring hope to your comrades."

"I was in complete control," said Comer, "I had full responsibility for my crew, and no one messed with me and my crew. We had a major who was a first class horse's ass, and one day he came down trying to boss me around and find out how well my crew could shoot. Right as he was berating us, a red warning sounded. We all jumped in the gun pit to ready the guns and do you know what that coward did? That Major hopped in his jeep to run away! One of my men, he climbed up on the embankment and pointed his rifle right at the Major's face. 'NO!' I yelled, because I knew if he killed that major, he would be court martialed and executed. It startled him and he shot out the windshield, but missed the Major. The Major kept going, and ran away. But nothing was ever said about it, and my man never got reprimanded."

I smiled at this good man, this kind man who had had to do some very horrible things.

"Comer, *you* were the one who gave your crew the window view day after day. How did you manage?"

Comer looked at me with glistening eyes, and his voice broke as he said, "A Colonel came to visit me one day, He would make periodic visits. He knew how that lieutenant had blocked my promotion for all those years. He told me, 'Comer, I wish there was a medal for keeping the morale of the men up the way you do.' "

"Even though you knocked a few heads?"

"You had to knock heads," he said, "It was expected. As an acting Sergeant, if I wanted to whack them, I could whack them. They never punished me, though they could have a thousand times over. I never hit anyone out of malice. I hit them because they weren't doing their duty."

Turning Points * Vicky Kaseorg

And they loved him. His men all huddled about him in the trenches loved him for the vision he kept before them.

"There's only one thing I was ever sorry for," said Comer, head bowed, "It's a story I don't think I told you yet."

I knew *this* was the story he had had on the tip of his mind since the interviews started. The one he could never remember. This was the dirty brick wall, blocking Comer's view. Another turning point...

"There was a new recruit from NY. I knew from the moment he came he should never have been a soldier. One day, we had a red warning. Everyone went to the gun pits and when the bombs started falling, we all jumped in the slit trenches. When it was all over, the new recruit was huddled in the corner, like a little cocoon, shaking. Just seeing me was enough to make most soldiers take courage, but this little fellow was half out of his mind with fear. I told him gently, 'It's over, get out, soldier.' But he just huddled in the corner. He wouldn't budge. I knew he wasn't coming out, shaking and muttering like an animal in the corner. So I pointed my machine gun in the opposite corner and fired some shots. I was trying to make him come to his senses. He lost his mind. They call that a 'section 8'. He went crazy. They had to cart him away to a mental institute and he never did recover. I always felt bad about that."

"You were trying to help him," I told Comer.

"Yes I was, but I didn't do the right thing. I made it worse."

"Maybe there was nothing anyone could have done."

"Maybe not," he said.

I glanced at my watch. It was after twelve. Comer had said he needed to get downstairs to help Evelyn with lunch at noon. I gathered my notes and stood to go.

"I would have ended the story a little differently," I said.

"Really? How would you have written it?"

"I would have had them move the soldier to a new room, with a window view, and this time, when he looked out, he would see the view he had always dreamed about and hoped for was there after all."

"Why would you end it like that?" he asked.

"Well, because I believe that there is hope, that there is redemption. That God is there. That the view represents good, and the corner, darkness and evil. And all of us are a mix of both, but all of us long for the light, for the view of hope. I believe God is real and I believe He promises us that one day we will look upon Him and all the horror and struggle of life will pass away."

"I look at Mama downstairs," said Comer, "And all those people out of their minds, and I wonder how could God allow that? Why does He make us suffer?"

"Well, I don't know, but I have my theories."

Comer looked intently at me, and asked, "What do you think? I used to be such an active man. I could do anything. Look at me now. I can barely walk across the room. Why?"

"This is just my idea," I said, "I can't answer your question completely. What I do know is that if life is too pleasant, too comfortable, too easy...we tend to ignore God. We feel we don't need Him. We are completely content without Him."

"That's true," said Comer.

"None of us would long for heaven if life was perfect here on earth. But God created us to be with Him. He wants us to desire His presence. I think struggle, and aging, and despair can sometimes drive us back to Him."

"That's true too," said Comer, "There are no atheists in a foxhole. But that whole description of heaven, streets paved in gold...I just don't know."

I laughed, "I just figure if you believe God created the universe, the God who made Jupiter, and Mars and all the planets and all the stars...He can do anything. Once you believe that...everything else is simple to believe."

"I see that," he said smiling, "That makes sense."

I hugged my old friend goodbye and drove home.

****

I called Comer the next week to see if he and Evelyn felt like joining me for a fast food lunch while sightseeing.

"Hiyah Sugar," he said, his voice weak, his speech slow and slurred, "I'm not feeling so good."

"You don't sound well," I said, "What is wrong?"

"Well, I collapsed yesterday, my body just gave out. I was on that cold hard floor for three hours before anyone found me. Spent the day in the hospital. All my vitals are good...I'm just terribly weak."

Turning Points * Vicky Kaseorg

"Oh my," I cried, "I am so sorry! Do they know what is wrong?"

"It's just my time," he said, "My body is just worn out."

I told him we would be gone the next two weeks on vacation, but when I returned, I prayed he would be feeling chipper again, and we could go out then.

"I hope so," he said, "I will see you then." Then he paused, and added, "God bless you, Sugar." I had the awful feeling Comer was saying goodbye permanently.

****

Vacation was wonderful, and then we returned home to one of the worst heat waves in our city's history. I sat listlessly in my living room. I rubbed my head and looked vacantly at the pretty flowers on the table in front of me.

Those beautiful purple flowers looked so real that they fooled everyone. What I loved about my lovely purple flowers was, unlike real flowers, they would not wilt or perish. Oh, how we humans long for permanence!

I had called Comer earlier that week when we first got back, and he was still doing poorly. I told him I would check on him in a few days and prayed he would be feeling better. But now, I felt a strong prompting to call Comer right away.

"I thought I would expire on Tuesday," he told me, "My organs are all fine, but I am just so weak, can't even get out of bed. What really bothers me is our book. I told my daughter, I would sure like to read my book! What if I don't last long enough to read Vicky's book about me? But my daughter said, 'Daddy, you *ARE* the book. You lived it. Don't worry about the book.'"

"Comer, the rough draft is done, or nearly done. It is very rough, no editing but if you like, I can copy that much for you so you can read it. Just remember, it won't be in its final form or nearly as good as it will be when I rework it."

"I trust you," he said, "If I should pass, you just use your imagination and you finish it as you see fit."

I wrote myself a note to copy the book and bring it to Comer in the morning.

"Well Comer, you rest, and I will call tomorrow to see if you are feeling better, ok?"

I was about to hang up, when he said, "Vicky, there's something I need to know."

"Yes?"

"Should I still trust in Jesus?"

Where did that come from? I sensed here was another turning point, perhaps the most important one yet.

I understood the question. Here was an old man, with a wife dying of Alzheimers. He had been a vital, strong man and his own mind was still sharp and alert. His wife still needed him, and his body had failed him. *Lord, give me words....*

"Comer, above all else, still trust in Jesus."

"My prayers don't seem to be working," he said.

"I don't claim to have any great knowledge," I told him, "But this is what I think. God is good. He has proved that to me, and to you, over and over again. Think of how many miraculous times he preserved you in the war. I believe He was saving you for a purpose. You have lived a long and fruitful life. Every one of us clings to the desire for youth, and strength, and vigor, but every one of us will feel our body fail. Our friends will fail us, our family will fail us. In the end, the only thing that will stand firm is our faith in Jesus, and His promises will not fail. You will stand before Him with a new body, healed of all sadness and disease and struggle, and Evelyn will be there with you. No

Alzheimers in Heaven! I often wonder what age we will be in Heaven, but I like to think that we will be whatever our favorite age was here on earth. I understand that right now, it doesn't feel like God is good, but if you think over your life, I will bet it was during the times of the most struggle that you matured and changed the most."

"That is true," he said. He looked at me intently, his hands clasped on his lap. He waited expectantly, as though whatever I had to say really mattered right now. Comer wanted very much for me to continue.

"Like when you didn't pass the Bar exam, I remember you telling me how devastated you were. But in the end, it made you take a completely unexpected career path, and it was the best thing that ever happened to you."

"You are right about that!"

"I think there are two responses to struggle, and trials. We can become bitter and angry and rail against God, and abandon Him. Many people do that. Or we can trust that there is a purpose in all our trials, though we may not always see or understand the purpose. We can trust that God is good, and all things that happen will ultimately lead us to the best place we should be. I think if God let us remain young, and strong, and filled with all the beauty and skill of youth, none of us would long for heaven. But this body was never meant to be permanent. Earth was never meant to be our final home. It is when we grow old, and weary that we long to move on to a better place. It doesn't feel like a kindness from God, but I believe it is. I think it is our struggles that make us lean on Him and trust Him. We will lose everything else, but we won't lose Him. And in the end, we will have all the best. At least, this is what I believe to be true."

"I am so glad I spoke with you," said Comer, sitting back against the cushion, "I was feeling mighty low, and I wondered if I should still trust Jesus. But what you are saying, it makes sense."

"I think of how so often my children didn't like what I made them go through, or my rules, or the consequences of their behavior," I continued, "At times, I know they felt I was cruel. To them, it felt cruel not to have all the ice-cream they wanted, or horror of horrors- limited computer time! But with my experience and age and greater vision of the whole of their life, I knew what was needed better than they did with their limited perspective. What felt to them like cruelty was in fact my greatest moments of love and kindness. God is our heavenly Father. He has a perspective we cannot have, and He loves us. If nothing else, still trust in Jesus."

"I promise you, I will," said my old friend with more strength in his voice.

When I hung up the phone, I sat down with a heavy heart. The beautiful purple flowers greeted me, the fake flowers that looked so real but whose petals would never droop. On the other hand, they also would never smell as intoxicatingly sweet as the flowers of the field. I opened my Bible and read the verse from Genesis, after Jacob wrestled with God all night:

Genesis 28:15-17 (NIV)
I am with you and will watch over you wherever you go, and I will bring you back to this land. I will not leave you until I have done what I have promised you. "[16]

When Jacob awoke from his sleep, he thought, "Surely the Lord is in this place, and I was not aware of it."

[17] He was afraid and said, "How awesome is this

place! This is none other than the house of God; this is the gate of heaven."

That had been the turning point for Jacob, who in the struggle with God was renamed, "Israel."

****

I copied the rough draft of the book for Comer and brought it to him the next afternoon. He was bundled in blankets, sitting up in a recliner. His door was open and the light by his chair was on, but his eyes were closed. Beside him was another chair, with a pillow on it.

"Comer?" I said.

He opened his eyes.

"Oh hello, Darling!" he said weakly.

I hugged him. He felt fragile, and hot.

"I brought the draft of my book," I told him, "I thought it would help pass the time while you are not feeling well." I pointed at the chair with the pillow on it,

"Is that for Mama?"

"Yes," he said, "She was just here."

I was glad the nurses were bringing Evelyn up to see Comer.

"Still not feeling so well?" I asked.

"No," he said shaking his head, a crooked smile tugging ever so slightly at one corner of his mouth.

"Well remember, this isn't edited and it isn't in its final form, but I thought you would want to see it. You can tell me how accurate it is."

A nurse came in and I noticed her tag identified her as a hospice nurse. I knew that meant that she was there to be sure Comer remained comfortable, but that I was not the only one that felt Comer was preparing to say a final goodbye.

She asked him some questions, and as she was leaving, I walked her to the door. Turning to me, she said, "I am glad to see he is feeling a little better."

"He is very proud of this book about him," I whispered, "I think it helps."

"I know it does," she said, "I have heard all about it!"

I returned to Comer who had flipped through some pages and then set the book down. He looked tired.

"I will call and see how you doing. You let me know if you find any mistakes in my book, ok?"

"Ok Sugar," he said. I hugged him, felt the heat rising from his scalp and quietly closed the door behind me.

The next day, I called to see if he was feeling any better.

"I started your book," he told me, "But I couldn't get very far. My eyes just can't focus. I can only read a minute or two, and they go all blurry."

"Would you like me to come and read to you?" I asked.

"Oh that would be wonderful!" he said, "Angie came and read to me a little. I would surely enjoy that!"

So I hurried over. When I arrived, Comer was sitting in the recliner again, burrowed under his blankets.

I pulled my chair close to him so he could hear and began reading. His listened with rapt attention, his eyes on me, his posture motionless. Sometimes he would nod, sometimes laugh, occasionally dash away a tear.

"I didn't expect it to be so exact!" he said.

"Well I recorded you, remember? And I took careful notes. I wanted to tell it exactly as you told it to me. Is that how you wanted it done?"

"Write it just the way you told me," he said smiling.

****

I returned the next day to read some more to Comer.

His door was closed, but I could see through the little window that opened onto the Senior Home hallway that his light was on and he was sitting in his recliner. I knocked, but I doubted his aged ears could hear, so I squeaked open the door a crack.

"Comer?" I called. He had been expecting me. I had promised to be there to read some more chapters of the book the day before. He was growing weaker by the moment, and I knew I might have little time to finish reading it to him.

Comer turned his head and looked dispiritedly at me.

"Comer, how are you?"

"Not good," he said breathlessly.

"Do you need a nurse?" I asked, frightened.

"No," he said, "I am fine. Just so weak."

"Do you want to rest? I can come back another time..."

"No," he said, "I'd like you to read to me."

"Well great then! I will just take over from where we left off yesterday."

He smiled wanly, and then his face assumed the same serious concentration I had seen the day before as I told him his story.

This chapter was particularly poignant. It was about the mirage of the submarine, which I considered a miracle, one of many. He had not called them miracles at the time, but they were pretty spectacular in my mind. While I was reading, his daughter, Angie came in. I knew she had been dropping by every day to see Comer, and I knew there was nothing that made him happier.

"Keep reading," she said, "I need to unpack some things into Daddy's fridge."

I read, a little self consciously, since this was one of the chapters where we discussed God. I was recounting the exchange Comer and I had had during the war interviews when he had asked me why Jesus had to come. I knew Angie was listening, and hoped she didn't think I was some wacko prowling for a deathbed conversion. Comer was a believer, and this discussion that I was now rereading to him had taken place months ago.

Just maybe, I thought, God intended the worried daughter to hear these words too....And there was no way she could miss them. I was almost shouting as I read, as that was the only way Comer could hear me.

When I finished the chapter, with my conclusion about Jesus, Comer smiled at me.

"Maybe we should break here," he said, "Angie hasn't much time, and I'd like to visit with her."

"Absolutely!" I said, "I can come back tomorrow if you like. We just have two more chapters to go. Would you like that?"

"I surely would," he said.

I left, and now with an open afternoon I had cleared for Comer, took my kayak and headed to the little quiet lake I loved. I was the only one there, as I unloaded my kayak and glided onto the peaceful water. I was feeling melancholy, and this lovely quiet lake was just what my soul needed. Two more chapters. I suspected that when I had finished the chapters, Comer would be finished as well. I felt a great weight of sadness.

It's funny, I felt afterwards that I had prayed the whole hour I was on the lake, but I don't recall really any intentional prayer. The lake was my prayer. The beauty of God's world touching my aching heart was my prayer. The still waters, singing birds, and curious turtles popping their heads up around my boat were my prayer. Together, without even knowing it, we were bathed in the mercy and glory of God. If one listened

Turning Points * Vicky Kaseorg

carefully enough, all our stories were being whispered in the wind, moaning to Heaven like a prayer.

I knew Comer's desire was that he hear all his stories in the book. Just two chapters to go. I called him again in the morning and asked if he wanted me to come right away or that afternoon.

"Now," he said. I knew 'now' might be all that was left to him.

I hurried over and found him in his recliner, covered with blankets. He could barely muster a smile.

"Are you ready to hear the last two chapters of your story?" I asked, settling into my 'reading chair.'

"Ready," he said quietly.

As I began to read, he closed his eyes. I wasn't even certain he was awake. But I kept reading. If he sleeps through it, I will just read it again, I thought to myself.

However, then I hit a very grim story, perhaps the grimmest of all, and he opened his eyes. It was the story of the soldier who went crazy when Comer fired his gun in the slit trench. His face looked very sad, and very serious. I knew the end of the chapters about him had a hopeful, triumphant passage, a cathartic turning point...but I wondered if I was doing the right thing reading through this deeply troubling section. When I came to the line that always makes me cry (I often move myself to tears with my writing), I saw his face contort and both of us were then choking back sobs. I read with a breaking voice. Then I came to the triumphant conclusion that God was, and always had been there. We reached the end of his stories. He smiled at me as I closed the book. I had worried he would tell me to strike out the grim section, perhaps even scrap the whole project. I held my breath, awaiting his verdict.

"I like it very much," said Comer.

I released my breath, "You see why I had to write it that way?"

"Yes I do," he said, "It is a work of art....What a wonder. I didn't think I would ever get to hear our book."

"I can read more if you like," I said, "Anything you want to hear."

"No," he said, "I am very tired." He leaned his head back and sighed deeply.

"Well then I will leave you to rest," I said. But I took his hand and asked if I could say a prayer with him.

"I'd like that," he said.

I prayed for his comfort, his peace, and thanked God for the time we had spent together. His eyes were already closing as I tiptoed away.

The following day, I called to see if perhaps he would want me to come read something else, to help him while away the hours.

"I would enjoy that," he told me, "I would really like you to read the short stories I wrote...if only I can find them."

So I headed back to the Home, and knocked on his door. He looked a little less peaked, and told me he had had a little breakfast. However, he had been unable to get out of his recliner to look for the short story he had written.

"Perhaps I could direct you," he told me. I looked in all the drawers he pointed me to, but the stories were not there. And then I noticed a briefcase beside his dresser. I brought that to him and he popped it open. There they were! The two short stories that Comer had first mentioned to me over a year ago.

"Please read them," he said, laying his head back against the cushion of the chair.

Turning Points * Vicky Kaseorg

One story was about a man who becomes marooned on an island. He goes about trying to survive, and weeks pass, and then a plane passes over the island. He tries to summon the plane, but it disappears and he knows that was his last chance for rescue. So he spends his days writing his life story. Once it is completed, he decides to summarize his life, and decides to do so by removing a page a day. Soon he is down to just one page. Then he removes words one by one, until he is left with just one word.

I looked up and he pointed to me, "And you can finish it any way you like. The next page is my word."

I flipped to the last page of the story to see Comer's word.

"Regret?! That is how you sum up your life!" I cried, "Regret!?"

"Yes," he said.

"Still? Now? When did you write this story?"

"Many years ago...but yes, I would still use that word. But it isn't how I would sum up my life. It is more like at the end of a life, what you wish you could take back. Read the list."

I looked at the page. Under the word 'regret' was this list:

Regret: to lament or stress over a desire unfulfilled or an action performed or not performed.

I regret many things I did.
I regret many things I did not do.
I regret all my sins.
I regret all my wasted hours.
I regret my lack of appreciation.
I regret my inconsiderations.
I regret my short sightedness.
I regret the error of my ways.
I regret my inability to make amends.
I regret my lack of understanding for weakness.
I regret my untempered violence.
I regret my wrong decisions.
I regret my lack of forgiveness.

"I see," I said, "I regret all those things in my life too. You know, everyone has these regrets. It is why the Bible tells us that we all fall short of the glory of God."

"Exactly," he said, "It was really not the summing up of my life, it was that as you look back as an old man over your life, you peel away one by one all the things you didn't realize before. You see the truth of what you are and what you were. In a way, it is my apology to God."

"I see that," I said, "But you were more than regrets. Surely you must also look back and see the good, the positive, the contribution you made. If all you look back and see are regrets, what is the purpose of living?"

"Yes," he said, "I agree. If I had to label the positive side in one word it would be 'zest for life'."

"That *does* describe you Comer," I laughed, "But that is *three* words. What would the *one* word be now, the purpose of your life?"

He looked at me and his hands were busily smoothing out the blanket on his lap, lifting it to gently shake out the wrinkles and then placing it again across his thighs.

Finally he answered, "God."

The final turning point, and the best one, since all of eternity creaked on that hinge.

Turning Points * Vicky Kaseorg

The Turning Point

by

Comer Hawkins

The Milne Bay Battle which was
So Horrible and sad is over.
But there will be no blue birds over
The white cliffs of Dover.
Just memories of brave and glorious
Young men
Who fought and died for their country
And if ever necessary, would do it again.

Where is the glory of war?
Death, where is thy sting?
The price is high; the benefits small.
I pray this be the last one
But then, don't we all?

Let God be your leader
Let Him hold your hand
Down the path of the parted sea.
Have faith, and trust, and love the land.

Selected Bibliography

1. "HyperWar: US Army in WWII: Victory in Papua." HyperWar: US Army in WWII: Victory in Papua. Samuel Milner, n.d. Web. 17 Aug. 2012. <http://www.ibiblio.org/hyperwar/USA/USA-P-Papua/USA-P-Papua-5.html>.

2. Casey, Hugh J., ed. (1951). Airfield and Base Development. Engineers of the Southwest Pacific. Washington, D.C.: United States Government Printing Office.

3. Centers for Disease Control and Prevention. Centers for Disease Control and Prevention, 08 Feb. 2010. Web. 17Aug.2012. <http://www.cdc.gov/malaria/about/facts.html>.

4. "Fata Morgana (mirage)." Wikipedia. Wikimedia Foundation, 13 Aug. 2012. Web. 18 Aug. 2012. <http://en.wikipedia.org/wiki/fatamorgana(mirage)>

Other books by Vicky Kaseorg

I'm Listening With a Broken Ear
God Drives a Tow Truck
Tommy - A Story of Ability
The Good Parent
The Illustrated 23rd Psalm

Books by Comer Hawkins

Comer Lafayette's Poems- Vol. 1 and 2

Turning Points * Vicky Kaseorg

What the Reviewers Say

If she writes it, I read it., August 29, 2012

By Luana Marler -

This review is from: Tommy- A story of Ability (Kindle Edition)

What a wonderful book! I loved every minute of it. She writes beautifully and anyone that is an animal lover (or even an animal "liker") will love this book. She has a way with words that leave all of us feeling better when we've read the book. From the time this little puppy was sent down the shute to become available for adoption until....oh, never mind, I don't want to give it away.....the story held my interest.

I highly recommend this book - and any other she has written!

5.0 out of 5 stars I learned, I cried, I was inspired, I was intrigued and entertained!, August 17, 2012

By J. Stacy Crawley

This review is from: I'm Listening With a Broken Ear

I enjoyed her novel God Drives a Tow Truck, so I immediately read this book as as follow up. I was not disappointed. I laughed out loud, so many times;my husband was constantly asking me what was so funny. I also cried, out of realizations made in my own life, taught so well by such a delightful author. I will recommend this book and the other to everyone I know, and I must say; I have been gifted with the ability to spread the word. Spreading the word of christ is made more simple by books such as this. You go girl! You've raised good kids, taught them and yourself lessons along the way, you have a generous spirit, and are beloved by God. Thank you for writing, it undoubtedly made my life better having read your work and I will pray that others will be blessed as well!

Richard French (Fort Lauderdale, FL USA) -

Vicky's writing style contains dry humor, sarcasm, and tons of introspection. She comes across as highly intelligent, caring, and honest. So between her qualities and her style, the result is a very good book. But more importantly, because of her compassion, a dog received a second chance even though it was a tough battle. I applaud Vicky for her and her daughter's perseverance.

Humor and honesty - a great rescue dog read, July 11, 2012

By Korrigan "korrigan" (Australia) -

This review is from: I'm Listening With a Broken Ear (Kindle Edition)

This lovely book abounds with characters to cheer on - Vicky, her daughter Asherel, rescue dog Honeybun, Malta of Last Chance Rescue - each of them on their own journey. Vicky and her daughter rescue a sick abandoned stray dog and so start an amazing year. This is not a sickly sweet book about the perfect rescue dog - Honeybun is certainly challenging and it takes a tough dog expert to guide Vicky and Asherel into the right training for this dog. Vicky who hopes eternally for quick fixes and ego boosts learns some hard won lessons, while eleven year old Asherel works with quiet determination, grace and perseverance towards her own goals. This book deals with the reality of coming face to face with our own failings of character, financial difficulties, the truly tough and heart breaking world of animal rescue and how people must take responsibility for their actions and find their own solutions. This is not a grim read, it is written with a light hand and much humor and honesty. My only warning is that this book does rest heavily on Christian doctrine, and while done with a gentle touch and much good humor, this aspect may not work for everyone. Still, this title has made it into one of my top five 'dog books'. I salute the author and toss Honeybun one of her beloved meatballs.

Made in the USA
Lexington, KY
06 December 2012